T0328602

Cambridge Elements

Elements in Magic
edited by
Marion Gibson
University of Exeter

WITCHCRAFT AND PAGANISM IN MIDCENTURY WOMEN'S DETECTIVE FICTION

Jem Bloomfield
University of Nottingham

CAMBRIDGE
UNIVERSITY PRESS

CAMBRIDGE
UNIVERSITY PRESS

University Printing House, Cambridge CB2 8BS, United Kingdom

One Liberty Plaza, 20th Floor, New York, NY 10006, USA

477 Williamstown Road, Port Melbourne, VIC 3207, Australia

314–321, 3rd Floor, Plot 3, Splendor Forum, Jasola District Centre, New Delhi – 110025, India

103 Penang Road, #05–06/07, Visioncrest Commercial, Singapore 238467

Cambridge University Press is part of the University of Cambridge.

It furthers the University's mission by disseminating knowledge in the pursuit of education, learning, and research at the highest international levels of excellence.

www.cambridge.org
Information on this title: www.cambridge.org/9781009073998
DOI: 10.1017/9781009072878

© Jem Bloomfield 2022

First published 2022

A catalogue record for this publication is available from the British Library.

ISBN 978-1-009-07399-8 Paperback
ISSN 2732-4087 (online)
ISSN 2732-4079 (print)

Witchcraft and Paganism in Midcentury Women's Detective Fiction

Elements in Magic

DOI: 10.1017/9781009072878
First published online: June 2022

Jem Bloomfield
University of Nottingham
Author for correspondence: Jem Bloomfield, jem.bloomfield@nottingham.ac.uk

Abstract: Witchcraft and paganism exert an insistent pressure from the margins of midcentury British detective fiction. This Element investigates the appearance of witchcraft and paganism in the novels of four of the most popular female detective authors of the era: Agatha Christie, Margery Allingham, Ngaio Marsh and Gladys Mitchell. The author approaches the theme of witchcraft and paganism not simply as a matter of content, but also as an influence which shapes the narrative and its possibilities. The 'witchy' detective novel, as the author calls it, brings together the conventions of Golden Age fiction with the images and enchantments of witchcraft and paganism to produce a hitherto unstudied mode of detective fiction in the midcentury.

This Element also has a video abstract: www.cambridge.org/jembloomfield

Keywords: detective fiction, witchcraft, women's writing, magic in literature, paganism

ISBNs: 9781009073998 (PB), 9781009072878 (OC)
ISSNs: 2732-4087 (online), 2732-4079 (print)

Contents

Introduction

Witchcraft and paganism exert an insistent pressure from the margins of midcentury British detective fiction. Gladys Mitchell's *Come Away, Death* is dedicated to 'Evelyn Gabriel, whom Artemis bless and Demeter nourish; upon whom Phoebus Apollo shine'.[1] Ngaio Marsh's *Off With His Head* revolves around a folk dance when ritual words are muttered and a murder is committed. Margery Allingham's *Look to the Lady* depicts the spontaneous rebirth of witchcraft in the depths of the English countryside. The theme appears across the work of multiple writers, going beyond chance occurrence to constitute an ongoing concern in the fiction of the period. This Element investigates the appearance of witchcraft and paganism in the novels of four of the most popular female detective authors of the British mid twentieth century. I approach the theme of witchcraft and paganism not simply as a matter of content, but also as an influence which shapes the narrative and its possibilities. The 'witchy' detective novel brings together the conventions of Golden Age fiction with the images and enchantments of witchcraft and paganism to produce a hitherto unstudied mode of detective fiction in the midcentury.

Witches in the Landscape

To set the scene for an investigation of these 'witchy' detective novels, I position them at the intersection of two developments in social and cultural history during the British midcentury: firstly, the rapid development of witchcraft as a religious movement in this period, including the legal and social background; secondly, the shift to the 'domestic' and 'feminine' in British culture in the era. These contexts of change frame the witchy detective novel as a cultural phenomenon, which I then theorize by drawing on work by scholars including Maurizio Ascari, Michael Cook and Tzvetan Todorov.

The mid twentieth century saw dramatic changes in the discourses around witchcraft outside literature with two major flashpoints: changes to witchcraft laws and the emergence of witchcraft as a religious movement. The full title of the new law, appended to the parliamentary document of 22 June 1951, is 'An Act to repeal the Witchcraft Act, 1735, and to make, in substitution for certain provisions of the Vagrancy Act, 1824, express provision for the punishment of persons who fraudulently purport to act as spiritualistic mediums or to exercise powers of telepathy, clairvoyance or other similar powers'.[2] The text of the Act provides for a fine of up to fifty pounds and a prison term of up to four months

---

[1] Gladys Mitchell, *Come Away, Death* (London: Michael Joseph, 1937, repr. Penguin, 1954), p. 4.

[2] Available on the UK government's legislation.gov.uk website at www.legislation.gov.uk/ukpga/Geo6/14-15/33/enacted?view=plain+extent.

for anyone who 'with intent to deceive' claims to 'act as a spiritualistic medium or to exercise any powers' of the kind named in the title, or for anyone who 'uses any fraudulent device' whilst claiming to do so. It further specifies that the Act can only be used to convict someone who did so 'for reward' of money or other valuables and does not apply to 'anything done solely for the purpose of entertainment'. The Vagrancy Act of 1824 to which it refers labels as a 'rogue and vagabond' anyone 'pretending or professing to tell Fortunes, or using any subtle Craft, Means, or Device, by Palmistry or otherwise, to deceive and impose on any of His Majesty's Subjects'; a list of equivalent people includes those sleeping in barns or outhouses, showing their wounds to beg for money, betting in the street or carrying burglary equipment. Going back further, the Witchcraft Act of 1735 was itself a repeal of laws against witchcraft in the reign of James I. The 1735 Act stated that no one should be prosecuted for 'Witchcraft, Sorcery, Inchantment [*sic*], or Conjuration' and that further to this, it would be illegal for anyone

> to pretend to exercise or use any kind of Witchcraft, Sorcery, Inchantment [*sic*], or Conjuration, or undertake to tell Fortunes, or pretend, from his or her Skill or Knowledge in any occult or crafty Science.

This quick overview of the laws preceding the period studied here reveals a spectrum of attitudes towards witchcraft. The laws enacted under Tudor and Stuart monarchs punished witchcraft as a supernatural way of causing harm. According to the eighteenth-century law, witchcraft did not exist; instead what should be prosecuted was encouraging others to believe that one had supernatural powers. The nineteenth-century law treated witchcraft as a form of low-level antisocial behaviour which identified the practitioner as a vagabond living a disorderly and faintly criminal life. The Fraudulent Mediums Act of 1951 sees activities which claim a supernatural element as potentially harmful when used to deceive or extract money but also as containing the potential for honest and conscientious practice or for harmless entertainment. This Act thus moved the official attitude to claims of magical and psychic powers, placing them in the context of an increasingly liberal and pluralist religious outlook as a respectable practice for the believer and as a mild thrill for the knowing sceptic.

The new legal situation had its counterpart in the cultural movements towards the emergence of Wicca as a religion, detailed by Ronald Hutton in *The Triumph of the Moon*. In the early 1950s, a retired civil servant named Gerald Gardner, who had previously written novels about magic and been involved in the Rosicrucians and the Folk-Lore Society, publicly announced that there was a secret pre-Christian witchcraft religion called Wicca. He stated that it had been in continuous existence for centuries but had been kept secret for fear of persecution. He himself had been initiated into the religion in the late 1930s by a coven in the New Forest. Gardner established covens of Wicca in various places in Britain, and other forms of witchcraft religion also emerged in the following decades. Hutton emphasizes that pagan witchcraft, 'the only religion which England has ever given the world', may appear an odd and eccentric side road in historical study but it in fact brings together major themes and concerns in European culture stretching back to the Romantic movement.[3] His study traces (and questions) the history of Gardner's declaration that witchcraft was a mystery religion passed down the centuries by initiates only now to emerge publicly in the altered legal conditions. It also situates these events within a 'macrocosm' of attitudes towards paganism, magic, witchcraft and the past. For this Element it is significant to note that the arrival of pagan witchcraft as a religious movement, signalled by Gardner's books such as *Witchcraft Today* (1954) and *The Meaning of Witchcraft* (1959), can be read as a culmination of a broader cultural concern with witchcraft and paganism. This concern continued alongside the practice of Wicca (and other forms of witchcraft religion) by modern witches. The religion newly identified as Wicca by Gardner itself combined several strands. It was a religion in that it provided a set of beliefs in deities along with rituals and a liturgical calendar. It was a form of magic in that its practices included spells and charms intended to influence the world around the practitioner. It was witchcraft in that it identified the witches of early modern history as its forebears and claimed that they belonged to the same religious system. Wicca thus combined and focussed a variety of cultural and historical influences, including nineteenth-century ritual magic, records of witch trials and theories about a prehistoric Goddess religion. Those strands were also available to others in the period: as Hutton has noted, figures like Aleister Crowley and Dion Fortune produced other kinds of esoteric and magical systems. In literature, Marion Gibson has discussed the way Sylvia Townsend Warner reacted to Margaret Murray's theory about witchcraft being a prehistoric Goddess religion and how Murray's ideas both interested and repelled the novelist during the writing of *Lolly Willowes*.[4]

The novels discussed here thus were published during decades when ideas about historical witchcraft were flourishing in the public sphere and witchcraft itself was emerging as a contemporary religious movement. For the first time in British history, significant numbers of people were publicly identifying themselves as practitioners of witchcraft whilst controversies continued about its

---

[3] Ronald Hutton, *The Triumph of the Moon: A History of Modern Pagan Witchcraft* (Oxford: Oxford University Press, 1999, repr. 2001), p. vii.

[4] Marion Gibson, *Rediscovering Renaissance Witchcraft: Witches in Early Modernity and Modernity* (Abingdon: Routledge, 2018), pp. 62–3.

status and nature. This is not simply a historical backdrop to the detective novels I am investigating, but a sphere of cultural controversy in which they partici-pated. Robin Briggs' often-quoted phrase that witchcraft is a 'crime ... with a hole at the centre' provides a useful touchstone since historians of the early modern period must proceed on the basis that witches did not in fact do the things of which they were accused (and indeed to which they confessed in some cases).[5] This dictum could be extended in the early twentieth century to the effect that witchcraft was an idea with a hole in it, or, rather, a hole where a series of ideas met and contended. There was disagreement about whether witches (had) existed. As traced by Hutton, an older Enlightenment scepticism which saw them as a superstition of peasants and fanatical inquisitors was confronted by new theories which proposed that groups of witches had existed underground for centuries.[6] There were disagreements about whether witches were virtuous or evil. Writers like Montague Summers described them as practising black magic and worshipping Satan, whilst Murray represented them as innocent healers wrongly persecuted by the Christian church. The novels explored in the following sections drew on the competing contemporary ideas about witchcraft and presented their own particular visions of it.

In these works, witchcraft intersects with another significant contemporary moment. The interwar period in Britain saw a shift in social and cultural life which can be termed the 'turn to the domestic'. This has been identified and analysed by Alison Light in *Forever England: Femininity, Literature and Conservatism between the Wars*, in which she describes a 'strongly anti-heroic mood' in the period's culture.[7] This reaction to the war years, and the images of national identity which preceded them, led to a 'redefinition of Englishness' towards a national self-image 'at once less imperial and more inward-looking, more domestic and more private'.[8] Light argues that these values were coded as 'feminine', in pre-war terms at least, and that the shift in public culture intersected with the changes in gender roles during the interwar era. In her account, whilst women moved more into the workforce and the political sphere, the public realm shifted towards 'a new kind of Englishness' which could be seen to '"feminise" the idea of the nation as a whole, giving us "a private and retiring people"'.[9] This change registered, for Light, in the political and social attitudes of the nation as well, drifting towards the

---

[5] Robin Briggs, *Witches and Neighbours: The Social and Cultural Context of European Witchcraft* (Malden, MA: 2002, 2nd ed.), p. 7.

[6] Hutton, *Triumph*, pp. 132–50.

[7] Alison Light, *Forever England: Femininity, Literature and Conservatism between the Wars* (London: Routledge, 1991), p. 8.

[8] Light, *Forever*, p. 8.   [9] Light, *Forever*, p. 210.

conservatism which her title pairs with femininity. The 'female population . . . became . . . in some ways symbolically . . . the nation between the wars', and the attitudes which had constituted a conscious protest against pre-war gender and social conventions became 'a mode of settlement, a compromise which identified the national with the private and made the latter speak for the former'.[10] In *Forever England*, the retreat from imperialist rhetoric is associated with a 'feminising' of the public realm, a stress on private and 'suburban' virtues and an instinctive insular conservatism.

A similar connection between small-c conservatism and the 'feminine' was reached by Jessica Mann's *Deadlier Than the Male*. Subtitled *An Investigation into Feminine Crime Writing*, Mann's study sets out to answer the question 'Why is it that respectable English women are so good at murder?' She focusses on the fact that the work of Agatha Christie, Ngaio Marsh, Margery Allingham, Dorothy L. Sayers and Josephine Tey was not only wildly successful in a genre apparently concerned with death, but also 'survived as popular reading' beyond the work of their male contemporaries.[11] Whilst Mann notes that as a 'lifelong feminist' she is uneasy about emphasizing authorial gender in writing beyond 'the most objective differences', her argument hinges on the idea that 'these famous women crime novelists were conventional, conformist and conservative' and 'adherence to accepted standards in their fantasies' was key to their appeal for readers.[12] Mann links this conservatism to their experience as women, suggesting that 'in most women's novels, individual people are of major importance, both as victims and participants in events'.[13] She contrasts this concern with 'recognisable personalities' with novels that dramatize 'threats to groups, nations or the whole world' and grimly notes that women are 'not yet educated to waste regiments'.[14] This theme was carried further by Nicola Humble's study *The Feminine Middlebrow Novel 1920s to 1950s*, which drew on Light's work and identified a specifically 'feminine' mode of middlebrow writing in the era. All three critics are working from a feminist point of view and so emphasize that the category of 'feminine' is historically contingent both in itself and in its connection to conservatism (whether social or political). Nonetheless, they highlight an aspect of midcentury British culture visible in contemporary sources.

I describe it as a turn to the 'domestic' since that term encompasses the international/insular and public/private associations. It is both domestic as opposed to abroad and domestic as opposed to public. The term also nuances

---

[10] Light, *Forever*, p. 210.

[11] Jessica Mann, *Deadlier Than the Male: An Investigation into Feminine Crime Writing* (London: David and Charles, 1981), p. 9.

[12] Mann, *Deadlier*, p. 13.   [13] Mann, *Deadlier*, p. 241.   [14] Mann, *Deadlier*, p. 241.

the gendered associations of this cultural shift and the way 'feminine' can gesture towards values not obviously gendered. I argue that this development in midcentury British culture made witchcraft an attractive source of imagery since it was 'domestic' in both senses. It originated in Britain and scholars including Diane Purkiss have emphasized historical witchcraft's concern with fears embedded in the home, family and neighbourhood. Witchcraft, as it appears in the witchy detective novel, is part of an enchanted British landscape and takes place in the local and domestic arena. It excludes politics in the international or factional sense, distinguishing itself sharply from the imperial-sounding rhetoric of ritual magicians who purport to summon spirits from other realms and even to command armies of them. Its power is rooted in the kitchen and garden and its scope is intensely and deliberately personal. Witchcraft provided a language and imagery for midcentury detective novelists – especially the women whose works I investigate here – to articulate and explore the meaning of this social and cultural shift. This is not to reduce the witchy element in their work to a set of contextual drivers. Witchcraft was a real set of phenomena in the historical record and a real religious movement beyond fiction. In framing the witchy detective novel at the intersection of the witch-craft revival and the turn to the domestic, I do not mean to suggest that one explains away or cancels out the other. Rather, the combination provides a powerful explanatory matrix within which to explore what witchcraft meant in these novels.

The Double Vision

In presenting witchcraft themes and imagery, the midcentury detective novel could draw on two features fundamental to the genre: an ongoing dialectic between the rational and the supernatural, and a 'double vision' via which authors and readers were used to envisioning two parallel stories in one novel. I argue that these aspects of the detective novel allowed it to mediate witchcraft material in an especially effective and meaningful way for contemporary readers and that the resulting fictional mode maps onto the mindset of modern pagan witchcraft.

Previous scholars have analysed the presence of non-rational or supernatural material within detective fiction, in terms of both the genre's origins in sensation fiction and its operations. Ascari's *A Counter-history of Crime Fiction* questions the assumed division by which the cerebral genre of detective fiction was supposedly created by the removal of sensational and supernatural elements. According to Ascari, although the 'association between detection and science might lead us to believe that nineteenth-century detective fiction was unambiguously realistic', it actually inhabited a much more 'ambivalent' mode of fiction.[15] He stresses the genre's continuing infusion of non-rational elements, especially on the level of tone and atmosphere.

> Like Doyle and Chesterton before her, Christie reduced the supernatural to the subsidiary role of transitory explanation, but at the same time she also exploited it to conjure up an ominous atmosphere of mystery that lures the public into reading and is progressively cleared away by the investigation.[16]

Ascari argues that Christie 'brilliantly condensed the two strands of crime and detective fiction in her apparently rational but actually gothic mysteries'.[17] Michael Cook's *Detective Fiction and the Ghost Story* develops the interest in the dialectic between rational and non-rational elements in a series of case studies. He even points out that the end of John Dickson Carr's 'The Burning Count' 'suggests that there are two solutions, one "natural", the other supernatural'.[18] He elaborates:

> The effective part of this *schema* is the way in which the underlying direction of the narrative is kept from view until the final page ... In doing so, Carr achieves the distinction of portraying the juxtaposition between these apparently irreconcilable genres. On the one hand lies logic, with its emphasis on cause and effect, and on the other, the realm of the metaphysical, which posits the impossibility of such reduction.[19]

Both critics, then, see non-rational and supernatural elements as part of the dynamic driving much detective fiction. Rather than framing the non-rational as a defunct part of the genre's history, they read it as part of the genre's DNA. It is carried by the form into the present and many of the genre's operations are enabled by this dialectic between the impossible and the realistic. We might even propose that the unrealized or suspended possibility of a supernatural solution – that an impossible situation might be explained via ghosts, psychic powers or magic – is one of the major drivers of the interest in much detective fiction. Thus, when witchcraft and paganism flowered so dramatically in the mid twentieth century, detective fiction already had an affinity for the supernatural.

The notion of an internal dialectic between divergent explanations for baffling events has been theorized for another mode of fiction in Todorov's *The*

---

[15] Maurizio Ascari, *A Counter-history of Crime Fiction: Supernatural, Gothic, Sensational* (Basingstoke: Palgrave Macmillan, 2007), p. xi.

[16] Ascari, *Counter-history*, p. 172.   [17] Ascari, *Counter-history*, p. 172.

[18] Michael Cook, *Detective Fiction and the Ghost Story: The Haunted Text* (Basingstoke: Palgrave Macmillan, 2014), p. 125.

[19] Cook, *Haunted Text*, p. 125.

Fantastic. He defines the fantastic as 'a certain hesitation' by reader and character in interpreting the meaning of a surprising event:

> In a world which is indeed our world, the one we know, a world without devils, sylphides, or vampires, there occurs an event which cannot be explained by the laws of this same familiar world. The person who experiences the event must opt for one of two possible solutions.[20]

The two solutions are to resolve in the direction of the 'uncanny', deciding that the event is odd but explicable by rational laws commonly agreed to pertain to the world, or in the direction of the 'marvellous', requiring the world of the fiction to deviate from (or add to) those laws. Todorov in fact discusses the detective novel, suggesting that some of Christie's work creates a potentially fantastic atmosphere (and that one Dickson Carr story achieves the true fantastic), but that

> The murder mystery approaches the fantastic, but it is also the contrary of the fantastic: in fantastic texts, we tend to prefer the supernatural explanation; the detective story, once it is over, leaves no doubt as to the absence of supernatural events.[21]

I wish to extend Todorov's notion of the hesitation between the uncanny and the marvellous into detective fiction itself and to argue that the witchy detective novel inhabits precisely this moment of the fantastic. In order to do so, I borrow another critical insight from Todorov. In his essay on *The Typology of Detective Fiction*, he identifies the dual nature of the detective novel: it 'contains not one but two stories: the story of the crime and the story of the investigation'.[22] He classifies these in Formalist terms as simply the 'fable' and 'subject' of all narrative fiction, but he insists that there is something unusual about their handling in this genre: 'How does it happen then that detective fiction manages to make both of them present, to put them side by side?'[23] Todorov's solution to this puzzle involves one story being 'absent but real' (the crime) and the other 'present but insignificant' (the investigation).[24] However, for the purposes of this Element, his crucial point is the paradoxical doubleness of the detective novel. It is a genre in which authors and readers are accustomed to hold two stories next to each other and observe the way the same events, people and physical items appear in both. I propose that this

---

[20] Tzvetan Todorov, *The Fantastic: A Structural Approach to a Literary Genre*, tr. Richard Howard (Ithaca, NY: Cornell University Press, 1973, repr. 1975), p. 24.

[21] Todorov, *Fantastic*, pp. 49–50.

[22] Tzvetan Todorov, *The Typology of Detective Fiction* (1966), repr. in Chris Greer, ed. *Crime and Media: A Reader* (London: Taylor & Francis, 2009), 'Reading 22', p. 3.

[23] Todorov, *Detective Fiction*, p. 4.   [24] Todorov, *Detective Fiction*, p. 4.

internal function of the detective novel enabled it to process witchcraft themes and images in a specific way, creating a fictional 'double vision'. This reading involves using Todorov's notion of the double form of detective fiction to extend the 'certain hesitation' which constitutes the fantastic. The works I discuss invite the reader to inhabit a fictional space in which events and outcomes can be explained by purely mechanical and rational means, or ascribed more mysterious and symbolic significance. Even framing this point in terms of causality and the sufficiency of evidence reduces it to a rationalistic model. It might be better to say that the pattern provided by events and characters in a given novel is meaningful when read as a diagram of empirical causes and effects, but equally so as a vision of bewitchings, charms and influences.

In elaborating the double vision presented by these novels, I connect them with the conceptual models advanced by scholars of modern witchcraft and magic. Tanya Luhrmann, in her landmark 1989 study *Persuasions of the Witch's Craft*, stresses the way contemporary witches and magicians inhabit two incommensurable mental worlds. She borrows the notion of incommensurability from the philosopher of science Thomas Kuhn, suggesting it could be useful because it posits a situation in which two languages or systems of interpretation could be used by two different groups to understand a set of phenomena, which would be both coherent and logical within their own terms, but incomprehensible to the other group. She adds that 'incommensurability becomes more perplexing in understanding contemporary magicians, because the witchdoctor and the scientist co-exist, as it were, within them'.[25] In Luhrmann's account, incommensurability and its problems give 'a clue to the nature of magical involvement and what I see as the ambivalence of the magician's belief'.[26] She identifies 'imaginative involvement' as crucial to the practices of modern magic and argues that this involvement permits 'systematic changes in the very structure of interpretation, in the sort of analysis which the magician brings to bear in making sense of any particular event'.[27] The system within which these interpretations are made is 'learnt, often informally, either through conversations or books', and Luhrmann notes that '[i]t is easy to forget that books are important socializing influences, if not more important than people' in the world of modern magic.[28] She emphasizes that the people she met during her study did not completely reject the world view of their society with its assumptions about

---

[25] Tanya Luhrmann, *Persuasions of the Witch's Craft: Ritual Magic and Witchcraft in Present-Day England* (Oxford: Blackwell, 1989), p. 325.

[26] Lurhmann, *Persuasions*, p. 325.   [27] Luhrmann, *Persuasions*, pp. 328, 313.

[28] Luhrmann, *Persuasions*, p. 313.

rationality and emphasis on technology. Rather, they developed another parallel system of interpretation whose tenets and claims they could indulge and explore at moments of intersection.

Sabine Magliocco echoes and develops this model in her 'New Age and Neopagan Magic'. She starts by positing that these movements involve a shift in the meaning of the word 'magic' in Western culture, that 'instead of implying surreptitious or irregular ways of controlling the natural world, it refers to a set of techniques for altering consciousness and bringing about personal transformation'.[29] Magic in New Age and Neopagan contexts, she states, affects the world insofar as it is a means of 'transforming human consciousness and creating a new perception of the world as sacred and enchanted'.[30] The central element of Neopagan magic, for Magliocco, can be identified in brief spaces of time when 'adherents have altered their consciousness, transforming themselves into deities and the ordinary world into a participatory, enchanted realm'.[31] Like Luhrmann, she insists that this does not involve completely abandoning a modern metaphysical system and substituting another: 'although Neopagan magic strives to re-enchant the world, it, too, is grounded in participants' experience of disenchanted modernity'. Where Luhrmann talks about involvement, Magliocco describes 'a degree of suspension of disbelief, of engrossment in a framed experience', as a necessity for the success of Neopagan magic. Both movements are 'quintessential products of modernity' and involve 'less rejections of rationality than creative responses to a disenchanted world in which personal spiritual experiences are both necessary to the human spirit and deeply distrusted by the dominant paradigm'.[32] Thus the approach to magic and reality scholars of modern paganism and magic describe maps onto the reading possibilities these novels offer. Crucially, it is not the content of magical belief which is mimicked by the witchy detective novel: it does not lay out explanations about the world of spirits or the operations of magic. Rather, it is the cognitive processes of indulging in magical belief which they offer as a reading experience. Luhrmann notes magicians reading lots of J. R. R. Tolkien and Ursula Le Guin, alongside works on tarot and witchcraft, whilst living in a technological world, and then holding within themselves the 'scientist' and the 'witch-doctor'. The witchy detective novel undertakes that metaphysical tension (if not synthesis) within itself.

---

[29] Sabine Magliocco, 'New Age and Neopagan Magic', in David J. Collins, SJ, ed. *The Cambridge History of Magic and Witchcraft in the West* (Cambridge: Cambridge University Press, 2015), pp.635–663, p.635.

[30] Magliocco, 'New Age', p. 633.   [31] Magliocco, 'New Age', p. 659.

[32] Magliocco, 'New Age', p. 659.

The Queens of the Witchy Detective Novel

Given the cultural history and theoretical model I have laid out, a refinement can be added to Todorov's model of the hesitation of the fantastic resolving itself into either the known world or the world of the marvellous. In this cultural context, there is some disagreement – or ambiguity – about what constitutes the real world. Tellingly, Todorov uses the phrase 'a hesitation common to reader and character, who must decide whether or not what they perceive derives from "reality" as it exists in the common opinion'.[33] Fiction which engaged with witchcraft and paganism in these decades held out another possibility since 'common opinion' was itself ambiguous. The texts offer the third possibility: that the reader neither resolve into the previously known world nor recognize the modification of that world within fantasy fiction, but indulge the idea that the known world's parameters might be blurred. This is only a possibility, and the novels are hospitable to a range of readings, but as witchy detective novels they are ideally placed to foreground questions of evidence, interpretation and meaning before holding the answers to those questions in tension.

The following sections examine appearances of witchcraft and paganism in the works of Christie, Allingham, Marsh, and Mitchell. I arrange the investigation by author since there are noticeable differences in the way these authors draw on the ideas and materials around witchcraft and paganism to develop their own individual emphases. Inside each section, I work chronologically since this reveals the arcs of development in some authors' work, which might be considered alongside the arrival and spread of Wicca and other forms of pagan witchcraft in public awareness.[34] Taken together, the works of these authors provide a coherent picture of the 'witchy' midcentury women's detective novel. Each displays a particular facet or aspect of that subgenre more strongly. Christie demonstrates a close and sustained engagement with major ideas and texts of witchcraft and paganism across the decades, from Murray to Gardner. Her novels track the changing notions of witchcraft's identity and substance in the twentieth century. Allingham depicts magic and witchcraft as part of an enchanted English landscape, presenting them as survivals from (or echoes of) the past centuries. Her novels take up the contemporary idea that archaeology and folklore could reveal 'pagan survivals' in rural culture and build it into a fictional dialectic which both ironizes and validates it. Marsh exemplifies a suspicion of occult and magical practices as debased forms of higher spiritual experiences. Her books are alert to the potential for esoteric religions to provide means for men to manipulate and dominate women, but increasingly

---

[33] Todorov, *Fantastic*, p. 39.
[34] A detailed account of this context can be found in Hutton's *Triumph of the Moon*, in the chapters entitled 'Wider Context: Reinforcement' and 'Wider Context: Hostility'.

suggest that there is a powerful, inarticulable mystery in the world. Mitchell continually calls her female detective a witch and offers a vision of witchcraft as a powerful and mysterious solidarity – even attraction – between women. Her characters are drawn into the landscape, by swimming or digging or other means, and, at moments of tragedy or idyll, are shown in mythical and magical terms.

1 Agatha Christie

Agatha Christie's novels present a sustained and varied engagement with major texts on paganism and witchcraft across the mid twentieth century. Her tendency towards textual echo, appropriation and rewriting allows precise parallels to be drawn between the passages of her books and their sources. In the case of the novels discussed in this Element, these sources range from J. G. Frazer's *The Golden Bough* and John Buchan's *Witch Wood* to Margaret Murray's *The Witch Cult in Western Europe* and Gerald Gardner's *Witchcraft Today*. Examining these parallels allows me to demonstrate that Christie's ideas about witchcraft and paganism are neither vague and ahistorical nor derived entirely from fictional material. Rather, they are in dialogue with the contemporary authorities on the subject and participate in the ongoing discussion over the nature of witchcraft. I contend that this is the case for all the authors covered here, but it is provable in a more precise and explicit way when dealing with Christie's novels. Whilst tracing these connections with texts on witchcraft and paganism, I examine the fictional uses Christie made of her borrowings. I demonstrate where she sets up the characteristic 'double vision' of the witchy detective novel. Christie's novels present patterns of events and symbols which are comprehensible as rational detective plots but also make sense as tales of enchantment and magic. These novels refuse to close the 'hesitation' of Tzvetan Todorov's fantastic and leave the reader with both a natural and a supernatural pattern. However, Christie eventually collapses this double vision in one of her late novels and insists on a rational solution which debunks witchy possibilities.

The Miss Marple story 'The Idol House of Astarte' (1928) provides a revealing example of Christie's handling of witchcraft themes at the early end of her career. The tale is framed as told by Dr Pender, a clergyman, and concerns 'a man stricken to death by apparently no mortal agency'.[35] It is introduced as showing that 'there are certain places imbued and saturated with good or evil influences which can make their power felt'; the place in question is a grove of trees near a house where a house party took place.[36]

---

[35] 'Christie, 'The Idol House of Astarte', in *Miss Marple: The Complete Short Stories*, (London: Harper Collins, 1997), p.17.

[36] Christie, *Marple*, p.17.

The bona fides of the grove are established by a tor nearby with 'hut circles, relics of the bygone days of the late Stone Age' and a barrow on another hill 'in which certain bronze implements had been found'.[37] The evidence points to 'Neolithic hut dwellers, Druids, Romans and even traces of the early Phoenicians', though the grove itself shows no such archaeological phenomena but is simply a 'densely planted grove of trees'.[38] When the clergyman expresses an unpleasant feeling walking through the grove, his host informs him that 'You are within your rights. This was a stronghold of one of the ancient enemies of your faith. This is the Grove of Astarte,' remarking that he prefers the 'Phoenician name of Astarte' to the other options, 'Ishtar, or Ashtoreth, or whatever you choose to call her'.[39] The host has built a folly there which he calls the Idol House, and it prompts the group to hold a party 'to celebrate the rites of Astarte'.[40] During the party, one of the guests (aptly named Diana) pretends to be a priestess of Astarte and threatens to strike down one of the other guests with magic when he approaches her; he falls over and is found to have been stabbed. It later turns out that the victim was stabbed impulsively by his cousin, who was in love with the same woman. The clergyman attributes this impulse partly to the wish to inherit estates which would allow him to marry Diana and partly to 'an evil influence in that grove'.[41] The last line of the story is Dr Pender's remark that '[e]ven to this day I can never think without a shudder of The Idol House of Astarte'.[42]

I pair 'The Idol House of Astarte' with Murray's *The Witch-Cult in Western Europe*. This anthropological work, published in 1921, was hugely influential on later notions of paganism, especially in its statements that early modern witch trials revealed a widespread pre-Christian religion focussed on the worship of the 'Horned God' Dianus and persecuted by the Christian church. This became a very popular idea, especially when coupled with the notion that prehistoric peoples had all worshipped a goddess whose instantiations included the Roman Diana and the Near Eastern Ishtar. This implied that patriarchal monotheisms had replaced a more female-centred and earth-focussed spiritual system. It became a foundational element in Wicca as a religious system. In Christie's story, Haydon's reference to the grove as a 'stronghold of one of the ancient enemies of your faith' picks up on the idea that Christianity was threatened by and sought to destroy the indigenous religious tradition which became the witch cult. As Murray put it:

> [T]he witches were believed to be possessed of devilish arts. As also every non-Christian God was, in the eyes of the Christian, the opponent of the

---

[37] Christie, *Marple*, p.19.   [38] Christie, *Marple*, p.20.   [39] Christie, *Marple*, p.20.
[40] Christie, *Marple*, p.21.   [41] Christie, *Marple*, p.33.   [42] Christie, *Marple*, p.33.

Christian God, the witches were considered to worship the Enemy of
Salvation, in other words, the Devil.[43]

Diana's suggestion that they have a 'moonlight orgy' (a phrase which connoted
more than specifically sexual enjoyment in the early twentieth century) connects with Murray's declaration that 'the feasts and dances – show that it was
a joyous religion' which was 'quite incomprehensible to the gloomy Inquisitors
and Reformers who suppressed it'.[44] Both Christie and Murray acknowledge
then mildly rebuke the association made between these rites and sexual licence.
Christie's Captain Rogers suggests that the sacred rituals were 'not very reput-
able by all accounts … rather hot stuff, I imagine', giving a 'loud unmeaning
laugh' to indicate to the reader his crassness and lack of insight. Murray
discusses the issue thus:

> The greater number of ceremonies appear to have been practised for the
> purpose of securing fertility. Of these the sexual ritual has been given an
> overwhelming and quite unwarranted importance in the trials, for it became
> an obsession with the Christian judges and recorders to investigate the
> smallest and most minute details of the rite. Though in late examples the
> ceremony had possibly degenerated into a Bacchanalian orgy, there is evi-
> dence to prove that, like the same rite in other countries, it was originally
> a ceremonial magic to ensure fertility.[45]

The persecutors of the witches and the modern man of the world are thus
bracketed together as unable to see beyond their own smutty view of the
world to the sacred fertility rituals (which happened to involve sex sometimes).
Diana's playing of the role of the priestess during the party and the accompany-
ing idea that she would have magical power to strike people down find a parallel
in Murray's statement that 'the deity of this cult was incarnated in a man,
a woman or an animal', whilst Diana's name itself has a significant echo:

> The feminine form of the name [of the god Janus/Dianus], Diana, is found
> throughout Western Europe as the name of the female deity or leader of the
> so-called Witches, and it is for this reason that I have called this ancient
> religion the Dianic cult.[46]

The name of the young woman – Diana Ashley – thus combines the 'Diana' of
the moon goddess, the 'Dianic cult' of the witch religion and the 'Ashtoreth/
Astarte/Ishtar' of the goddess religion. Christie does not mention the word
'witch' in 'The Idol House of Astarte' but it is clear how her version of
a pagan shrine in this story sits within the overlapping areas of the two strains

---

[43] Margaret Murray, *The Witch-Cult in Western Europe: A Study in Anthropology* (Oxford:
Clarendon, 1921, repr. 1962), p. 9.
[44] Murray, *Witch-Cult*, p. 15.   [45] Murray, *Witch-Cult*, p. 15.   [46] Murray, *Witch-Cult*, p. 12.

of contemporary thought about ancient goddesses and witches. The end of the story insists that, even once the methods and motivations of the killing have been explained, the narrator feels an 'influence' had been involved. The reader is offered a rational detective tale in which a desire for money and for love provides the motive for an apparently impossible (but actually completely explicable) murder. They are also offered a pattern of images which can be interpreted in magical terms: the young woman bearing the names of Diana and Ashtoreth is apparently inspired (or possessed) into claiming to be a goddess and causes a sudden death in the grove. The story thus sustains the hesitation of Todorov's fantastic moment throughout the entire text. The weight of the narrator himself is used to insist on the possibility of irrational meanings in the story. The result is a text in which Christie borrows from one of the classic works on paganism and uses it to construct the double vision of a witchy detective tale.

The novel *Murder Is Easy* (1938) develops the representation of paganism in 'The Idol House of Astarte' in two major senses. It sets several notions of witchcraft and paganism in dialogue with each other, distinguishing ritual magic from witchcraft and attaching moral freight to the distinction. It also develops the double vision element further, presenting a story in which characters (and potentially readers) experience events more explicitly as magical. Christie's novel begins by engaging with an earlier famous fictional representation of witchcraft: Buchan's 1927 *Witch Wood*. In Buchan's novel (itself influenced by Murray's *The Witch Cult*), a young Scottish minister arrives in a new village parish and gradually becomes aware that the locals still follow a pagan religion hidden throughout the centuries of Christianity. In Christie's novel, the village itself is called 'Wychwood-under-Ashe' and the young male protagonist (Luke Fitzwilliam) travels to it to investigate rumours of murder under the guise of investigating local folk customs and their connection to paganism:

> 'Now for your reason for going there – witchcraft, my boy.'
> 'Witchcraft?'
> 'Folklore, local superstitions – all that sort of thing. Wychwood-under-Ashe has got rather a reputation that way. One of the last places where they had a Witches' Sabbath – witches were still burnt there in the last century – all sorts of traditions. You're writing a book, see? Correlating the customs of the Mayang Straits and old English folklore – points of resemblance, etc . . . Go round with a notebook and interview the oldest inhabitant about local superstitions and customs. They're quite used to that sort of thing down there.'[47]

---

[47] Agatha Christie, *Murder Is Easy* (London: Collins, 1938, repr. HarperCollins, 2017), e-book, p. 21.

Thus *Murder Is Easy* does not so much echo or parallel *Witch Wood* as write back to it and build from it. The horrific secret which lurks at the centre of the remote community in Buchan's novel is so openly recognized and regarded as harmless that it provides the cover story for the investigation of something else in the later book. It also adds an elaboration to Buchan's title, calling the village 'Wychwood-under-Ashe' with the same echoes of 'Ashtoreth' audible in the name of Diana Ashley from the earlier story. It is worth noting that both Buchan's novel and Luke's cover story can be read within the 'turn to the domestic' outlined in the introduction. Buchan's book presents paganism as a mystery deep within Scottish history and culture, an exotic 'other' located inside the British Isles. The pretext which Luke's friend suggests has him moving from the British colonies to the heart of the English countryside. Both cast attention inward, in geographical and cultural terms, sitting within the turn away from the international and imperial rhetoric which Light defined.

Though Luke's avowed interest in paganism and witchcraft is only intended to deceive the villagers as to his real intentions, as soon as he arrives, he meets a woman whom he instinctively interprets as a witch:

> Her black hair was blown up off her head by the sudden gust and Luke was reminded of a picture he had once seen – Nevinson's 'Witch'. The long pale delicate face, the black hair flying up to the stars. He could see this girl on a broomstick flying up to the moon ... She came straight towards him. 'You must be Luke Fitzwilliam. I'm Bridget Conway.'[48]

For an audience familiar with midcentury ideas of paganism, it is hardly surprising that Luke interprets Bridget in witchy terms. Like Diana Ashley, her name signals her presence in two modes, since she shares a name with St Brigid of Kildare and with the pagan goddess Brigit. Both figures were celebrated on the first day of February, variously regarded as St Brigid's day and the pagan festival of Imbolc. The name, especially in a woman met in Wychwood-under-Ashe, invests her with a double image. Luke and Bridget's romance is depicted throughout the book in witch imagery, in lines such as 'He saw her black hair stream out behind her blown by the wind. Again that queer magic of hers held him. "Bewitched, that's what I am, bewitched," he said to himself.' When he comes to declare his feelings for her, the same phraseology appears:

> '[Y]ou came round the corner of that house and – how can I say it – put a spell on me! That's what it feels like ... You've bewitched me. I've a feeling that if you pointed your finger at me and said: "Turn into a frog," I'd go hopping away with my eyes popping out of my head.'[49]

---

[48] Christie, *Easy*, p. 25.   [49] Christie, *Easy*, p. 128.

The notion of a 'witch' appears here with a rather different cluster of associations than the antiquarian research in which Luke is pretending to be engaged. Purporting to make use of lore about witches, he finds himself drawn into the imagery himself, having experiences that can only be articulated via the language of bewitching and enchantment. Luke, as well as the reader, finds that magical imagery makes as much sense of the events in Wychwood-under-Ashe as rational or logical explanations.

The witch imagery in the novel is sharply contrasted with another version of magic, represented by the deeply unpleasant amateur artist and antique shop owner Mr Ellsworthy. Luke considers him a 'nasty bit of goods' with 'very unpleasant hands', whilst Bridget speculates that he has 'a nasty mind and nasty habits'.[50] When Luke asks, 'Why does he really come to a place like this?' she passes on rumours that 'he dabbles in black magic. Not quite black Masses but that sort of thing'.[51] The 'nasty habits' they refer to encompass having people down from London for the weekend to hold magical rituals and probably orgies, potential homosexual tendencies, and prattling on about art and life in a pretentious way. This latter habit is demonstrated in a passage which connects Ellsworthy with the 'decadent' and 'aesthetic' philosophies associated with Oscar Wilde, Walter Pater and Algernon Swinburne:

> 'I abhor Nature. Such a coarse, unimaginative wench. I have always held that one cannot enjoy life until one has put Nature in her place.'
> . . .
> 'Mens sana in corpore sano,' said Mr Ellsworthy. His tone was delicately ironic. 'I'm sure that's so true of you.'
> 'There are worse things,' said Luke.
> 'My dear fellow! Sanity is the one unbelievable bore. One must be mad – deliciously mad – perverted – slightly twisted – then one sees life from a new and entrancing angle.'[52]

It is crucial that Ellsworthy's comments about nature and perversion sound deliberately out of date: as well as portraying him as unpleasant, Christie has assigned him attitudes which were daring in the 1880s and 1890s, but familiar and threadbare decades later. Just as (in Light's account) the imperial and masculine-sounding rhetoric of earlier decades seemed discredited in the interwar years, the witchy novel sees Ellsworthy's brand of diabolism as outdated. Ritual magic is discredited by its lack of modernity as well as its tendency to corrupt.

Thus both the plot and the imagery use Ellsworthy to dissociate Luke's experience of being 'bewitched' from undesirable associations. That experience

---

[50] Christie, *Easy*, p. 61.   [51] Christie, *Easy*, p. 61.   [52] Christie, *Easy*, p. 103.

of Wychwood as a magical place becomes crucial in the denouement of the novel. When Luke first meets Miss Waynflete, who later turns out to be the murderer, her appearance prompts a simile in his mind: 'Her face was pleasant and her eyes, through their pince-nez, decidedly intelligent. She reminded Luke of those nimble black goats that one sees in Greece'.[53] Twice later he mentally refers to 'her intelligent goat's eyes' and 'her eyes – so like an amiable goat's'.[54] When Miss Waynflete has lured Bridget out to a cornfield with the intention of slitting her throat, the same image comes to the young woman's mind: 'How like a goat she is! A goat's always been an evil symbol! I see why now!'[55] The real locus of death and terror in the novel is shown to be Miss Waynflete, and both Luke and Bridget see her in terms of goat imagery. *Murder Is Easy* paints a landscape of rural England which Luke Fitzwilliam enters using folklore and witchcraft as a convenient excuse for his presence. The language and imagery of witchcraft, however, take over both his experiences and the atmosphere of the novel. The enchanting witch imagery associated with Bridget is set against the overt diabolism of Ellsworthy and the hidden evil of Miss Waynflete. Both the murder mystery and the romance plot are suffused with this imagery and, once the narrative is over, their effects remain. Luke has banished the influence of the 'goat' and ended up with the 'witch'. There is no attempt to explain away this language by the end of the novel and it remains Christie's most fully developed version of the double vision of the witchy detective novel.

The next novel I discuss inverts the approach taken in *Murder Is Easy*, moving from an English landscape with witchy undertones to an ancient pagan one with English echoes. Reading the book alongside Frazer's *The Golden Bough* allows me to draw out the threads of its engagement with magic and paganism. In 1944, Christie published her only historical detective novel, *Death Comes As the End*. It is set in ancient Egypt and centres on Renisenb, a young widow who has come back to her father's house to decide the future direction of her life. As part of this historical background, Renisenb and her grandmother Esa (a formidable English dowager transferred to the banks of the Nile) quote the wisdom literature of ancient Egypt. This is particularly explicit in one scene:

> 'No,' said Esa. 'The motive is more obscure than that. We have here either enmity against the family as a whole or else there lies behind all these things that covetousness against which the Maxims of Ptahhotep warn us. It is, he says, a bundle of every kind of evil and a bag of everything that is blameworthy!'[56]

---

[53] Christie, *Easy*, p. 53.   [54] Christie, *Easy*, pp. 56, 138.   [55] Christie, *Easy*, p. 236.

[56] Agatha Christie, *Death Comes As the End* (London: Collins, 1944, repr. HarperCollins, 2017), e-book, p. 226.

As Waltraud Guglielmi has pointed out, the *Maxims*, a major collection of gnomic sayings, were one of Christie's sources in constructing her historical background for the novel.[57] The collection also provides the quotation from which the novel is titled:

> 'Nofret is beautiful. But remember this: *Men are made fools by the gleaming limbs of women, and lo, in a minute they are become discoloured c[a]rnelians . . .* '
> Her voice deepened as she quoted:
> '*A trifle, a little, the likeness of a dream, and death comes as the end . . .* '[58]

The image of limbs turning to carnelian may well have prompted Christie to build part of the plot around a cheap necklace of carnelian beads. Within the novel, then, this material functions as setting, verisimilitude and potentially plot inspiration. However, knowledge of and interest in ancient Egypt was part of esoteric and magical culture in the early twentieth century. The Professor of Egyptology who translated and published the *Maxims*, Battiscombe 'Jack' Gunn, had been a member of the ritual magic group the Golden Dawn and had worked with Aleister Crowley on his religious system known as 'Thelema'. Gunn's translation of the *Maxims* appeared in a series entitled 'The Wisdom of the East'. Contemporary ideas about ancient Egypt were bound up with the culture's reputation for magic and occult knowledge. This aspect of the novel's setting becomes more evident when the characters discuss religion and the text begins a dialogue with *The Golden Bough*. Since the publication of its first version in 1890, Frazer's comparative study of anthropology, religion and magic had been one of the most influential books on the subject in Britain.

An explicit discussion of the nature of gods and religion takes place between Renisenb and Hori, the scribe whose proposal of marriage she will eventually accept. He declares that the culture of Egypt is underpinned by death, just as their household is maintained by the earnings of Renisenb's father as a priest who deals with death, and that 'We have no real belief in a God.'[59] Renisenb disagrees, listing the national gods, local gods, and gods connected with particular activities, but Hori asks:

> 'And what is the difference, Renisenb, between a God and a man?'
> She stared at him. 'The Gods are – they are magic!'
> 'That is all?'
> 'I don't know what you mean, Hori.'

---

[57] Waltraud Guglielmi, 'Agatha Christie and Her Use of Ancient Egyptian Sources', in Charlotte Trumpler, ed. *Agatha Christie and Archaeology* (London: British Museum Press, 2001), pp. 351–89.
[58] Christie, *End*, p. 54. [59] Christie, *End*, pp. 88–9.

> 'I meant that to you a God is only a man or a woman who can do
>   certain things that men and women cannot do.'
> 'You say such odd things! I cannot understand you.'[60]

Renisenb is articulating what the novel takes to be the accepted view of religion in ancient Egypt: that gods are patrons of particular areas or spheres of life whose favour can be exchanged for worship and offerings. Hori's questioning of this notion sets him up as a visionary figure seeing beyond the conventions of the past towards a new Egypt.

Reading across from *Death Comes As the End* to *The Golden Bough* provides some striking parallels. Frazer's discussion of the theological views of 'early man' includes these sentences:

> Nor does he draw any very sharp distinction between a god and a powerful
> sorcerer. His gods are often merely invisible magicians who behind the veil of
> nature work the same sort of charms and incantations which the human
> magician works in bodily form among his fellows.[61]

The idea that gods are 'magic', imagined simply as humans with supernatural powers, is expressed succinctly here. It is worth quoting a passage from the same discussion:

> Much of the controversy which has raged as to the religion of the lower race
> has sprung merely from a mutual misunderstanding . . . When the savage uses
> his word for god, he has in his mind a being of a certain sort: when the
> civilised man uses his word for god, he has in his mind a being of a very
> different sort.[62]

An ancient Egyptian may not be a 'savage' in the view of either Frazer or Christie, but the discussion just quoted maps exactly onto Frazer's account of the mutual misunderstanding between an earlier notion of gods as magic people and later ideas of them as metaphysically different beings. Renisenb herself comes to find the religion and mythology of her upbringing unsatisfying when she is faced with existential questions.

> 'What happens when you are dead? Does anyone really know? All these
> texts – all these things that are written on coffins – some of them are so
> obscure they seem to mean nothing at all. We know that Osiris was killed and
> that his body was joined together again, and that he wears the white crown,
> and because of him we need not die – but sometimes, Hori, none of it seems
> real – and it is all so confused.'[63]

---

[60] Christie, *End*, pp. 89–90.
[61] J. G. Frazer, *The Golden Bough: A Study in Magic and Religion* (London: Macmillan, 1922, abridgement, repr. 1932), p. 92.
[62] Frazer, *Golden Bough*, pp. 92–3.   [63] Christie, *End*, pp. 163–4.

The Golden Bough supplies a parallel passage:

> In the resurrection of Osiris the Egyptians saw the pledge of a life everlasting for themselves beyond the grave. They believed that every man would live eternally in the other world if only his surviving friends did for his body what the god had done for the body of Osiris.[64]

These textual echoes show Christie imagining the cultural and religious world of her characters through a text which was enormously influential on contemporary views of magic and paganism. As a piece of historical fiction, *Death Comes As the End* does not construct the witchy double vision I am investigating by placing two systems of interpretation in the same world. Rather, it depicts ancient Egyptian pagans whose world mirrors contemporary Britain in various ways: the sense of cultural exhaustion, the ubiquity of death, the desire for new spiritual insight. Where other novels of the era – such as her own *Murder Is Easy* – depict contemporary British characters who can be interpreted through the lens and language of paganism, Christie presents ancient pagans who can be interpreted through a contemporary lens. With this novel Christie continues her engagement with the classic texts of midcentury witchcraft and paganism, adding Frazer to Murray and Buchan in her list of sources. With the next book I discuss she produces a bleaker and more sceptical vision of the subject in a novel which provides echoes of Gardner's own *Witchcraft Today*.

The Pale Horse (1961) presents a supposed occult contract killing plot. It is rumoured in society circles that if a person wishes to arrange a death, they should get in touch with 'The Pale Horse'. This is revealed to be the name of a converted inn where three women live who claim to be able to cause death by performing elaborate rituals but without physically touching or even meeting the intended victim. The novel's hero works to expose the group by posing as a would-be client whilst the heroine pretends to be his intended victim. A great deal of the book is focussed on this occult group and their claimed powers, in contrast to the relatively quick denouement of the 'solution': they are simply a front for an inconspicuous man who introduces poisonous toxins into the victims' houses via toiletry products.

The witches of *The Pale Horse* are striking by their eclectic quality. Christie's presentation of them parallels Gardner's gathering various elements and labelling them as 'witchcraft'. The trio of women who live at the Pale Horse represent varying forms of magical, mysterious or supernatural forces. Sybil Stamfordis, whose name evokes the ancient seer, is a medium with 'lots of

---

[64] Frazer, *Golden Bough*, p. 367.

scarabs and beads' who tells fortunes at the village fete.[65] Bella Webb 'comes from the village of Little Dunning' and 'had quite a reputation for witchcraft', exerting powers described as 'a family asset that you inherit'.[66] Bella represents the traditional image of the witch as a threatening rural figure, and her killing of a cockerel suggests a connection between the demotic witchcraft of Britain and the practices of 'voodoo', more recently known to domestic readers. Thyrza Grey, described as 'very occult', is a magus in the ritual magic tradition, associated with learned magicians such as John Dee and the more recent Rosicrucian groups.[67] Her activities are classed as 'not quite black masses, but that sort of thing'.[68] The way these characters are characterized represents another shift in Christie's approach to the theme. In *Murder Is Easy*, ritual magic had been the preserve of the unpleasantly satyr-like Ellsworthy whilst Bridget had offered a positive image of a witch set within an enchanted landscape. Here witchcraft and ritual magic are bracketed together with a whiff of black magic and no redeeming enchantment. Indeed, it is when the female characters act like male ritual magicians that Christie undermines the entire possibility of witch-craft in her fiction.

When the protagonist witnesses one of their rituals, the same elaborate eclecticism is in evidence. The process involves a glove from the intended victim and a comment that 'the physical emanations from its wearer are quite strong'.[69] Sybil goes into a trance and has a spirit invoked into her whilst Thyrza and Bella place an inverted crucifix and holy water on her. Bella chants and sacrifices a cockerel and Thyrza activates some apparently secret technological device:

> It opened up and I saw that it was a large electrical contrivance of some complicated kind. It moved like a trolley and she wheeled it slowly and carefully to a position near the divan. She bent over it, adjusted the controls, murmuring to herself: 'Compass, north-north-east . . . degrees . . . that's about right.' She took the glove and adjusted it in a particular position, switching on a small violet light beside it.[70]

This scene emphasizes the connection between all forms of occult activity and implies that there may be some scientific and psychological process behind them. Thyrza remarks that

> I don't suppose you're much impressed, are you, by all the ritual? Some of our visitors are. To you, I dare say, it's all so much mumbo jumbo . . . But

---

[65] Agatha Christie, *The Pale Horse* (London: Collins, 1961, repr. HarperCollins, 2010), e-book, p. 49.
[66] Christie, *Pale*, p. 49.   [67] Christie, *Pale*, p. 48.   [68] Christie, *Pale*, p. 48.
[69] Christie, *Pale*, p. 196.   [70] Christie, *Pale*, p. 197.

don't be too sure. Ritual – a pattern of words and phrases sanctified by time and usage, has an effect on the human spirit. What causes the mass hysteria of crowds? We don't know exactly. But it's a phenomenon that exists. These old-time usages, they have their part – a necessary part, I think.[71]

She also refers to the combination of 'the old knowledge of belief, the new knowledge of science' and their lethal combination in the group's rituals.[72] The combination is then comprehensively inverted and debunked in the novel's denouement. The murders were actually committed via a rather mundane system of poisoning with the rituals simply providing distraction and cover. *The Pale Horse*'s plot argues that radio waves and death wishes are not genuine scientific principles which explain old superstitions, rather they are themselves modern expressions of superstition dressed up in pseudo-scientific language. As the protagonist exclaims: 'All that hooey! ... We don't believe in spirits and witches and spells nowadays, but we're a gullible lot when it comes to "rays" and "waves" and psychological phenomena.'[73]

The eclectic approach and the suggestion that witchcraft and emerging science have common ground are characteristic of one of the defining early works of Wicca: Gardner's *Witchcraft Today* (1954). Released two years after the change in the legal status of witchcraft (and seven years before *The Pale Horse*), it announced the religion of Wicca to the world and claimed the existence of covens which had survived centuries of secrecy. *Witchcraft Today* stresses the range of historical and contemporary forms of magic and paganism which it would classify as witchcraft, mentioning 'Voodoo', Egyptian magic and the activities of the Templars, and saying that today such practices would be classed as 'spiritualism, mesmerism, suggestions, E.S.P., Yoga or perhaps Christian Science: to a witch it is all MAGIC, and magic is the art of getting results'.[74] The three members of the Pale Horse similarly gather a range of traditions into their elaborately eclectic activities. The rationale for their ritual practice has a great deal in common with Gardner's account of how modern science and ancient beliefs are converging. The idea of sympathetic magic, he argues, would have been regarded as 'nonsense' and 'superstition' fifty years previously, but 'Nowadays, however, many scientific men believe that living tissues emanate their own radiations in conformity with their cellular structure.' Some people have 'a faculty ... of receiving waves or rays and passing them on through muscular reflexes to a divining rod or pendulum'; Gardner explains that this is the basis of dowsing and probably of the table-turning at séances. He claims that it is 'nowadays being investigated by a great

---

[71] Christie, *Pale*, p. 197.   [72] Christie, *Pale*, p. 197.   [73] Christie, *Pale*, p. 247.
[74] Gerald Gardner, *Witchcraft Today* (London: Rider and Company, 1954), p. 28.

number of medical men, priests and research workers', stating that '[w]e all know that wireless works, and this seems a sort of natural wireless'.[75] He also lays stress upon the psychological element of witchcraft: how ritual and practice draw out internal and natural sources of energy. Gardner describes a witch cult as producing 'a sort of human battery, as it were, of combined human wills working together to influence persons or events at a distance', and that '[t]o do this certain processes are necessary and the rites are such that these processes may be used. In other words, they condition you'.[76] This passage sounds exactly like Thyrza Grey's aforementioned comment about the potential of ritual words and actions to have an effect on human feelings. As a whole, the lines extracted from *Witchcraft Today* seem to be directly addressed by Mark Easterbrook in his condemnation of 'suggestion along the lines of scientific talk', which is simply modern superstition dressed up in phrases about 'rays and waves and psychological phenomena'.[77]

The vision of witchcraft Christie presents and critiques in the narrative of *The Pale Horse* is directly engaged with one of the foundational texts of Wicca at the time. Her novel reproduces distinctive elements of Gardner's portrayal of witchcraft, focussing on its wide historical claims as well as its combination of arcane belief, psychological language and scientific speculation. Within her novel, these are all subjected to scornful treatment as nothing more than ignorant superstition recast in language more appealing to the cultural vanity of a 1950s audience. There is no space in the novel for the kind of sympathy for historical paganism found in *Death Comes As the End* or for the indulgence of enchantment as a possibility in *Murder Is Easy*.

Conclusion

As I argued at the beginning of the section, these works demonstrate a close and focussed engagement with some of the most influential texts of modern paganism and witchcraft. Any writer whose fiction echoes Buchan's *Witch Wood*, Murray's *The Witch-Cult in Western Europe*, Frazer's *The Golden Bough* and Gardner's *Witchcraft Today* is engaged with the mainstream of magical ideas in the twentieth century. The echoes work to produce the characteristic witchy double vision in which the logical explanation and the consensus view of reality is shadowed by a set of magical images and patterns. This double vision grows out of detective fiction's ability to manage two 'stories' alongside each other (the story of the crime and the story of the investigation), but it also parallels the mental world of modern pagan witchcraft. I drew on Luhrmann's and Magliocco's work to argue that the two ways of interpreting the world visible

---

[75] Gardner, *Today*, p. 152.   [76] Gardner, *Today*, p. 28.   [77] Christie, *Pale*, p. 247.

in witchy detective novels map onto the conceptual structures of magic users themselves. However, as this section's examination of Christie's fiction shows, this does not necessarily mean that fiction hospitable to magical interpretation is also pagan propaganda. The texts I have explored take a range of attitudes towards actual paganism and witchcraft. 'The Idol House of Astarte' offers paganism as a possibility, but one which has disastrous results in the story. *Murder Is Easy* shows an enchanted vision of the world allowing crime to be solved and love to flourish, but it condemns ritual magic. *Death Comes As the End* presents ancient paganism as a mental and spiritual state with parallels to post-war Britain, but one which the characters need to transcend in order to have hope in the future. *The Pale Horse* shows contemporary eclectic ritual magic as cynical, meaningless and a cover story for a male killer.

These ambiguities become clearer by reading the novels in the light of the turn to the domestic in midcentury culture. Ritual magic is disclaimed in the novels and this aligns with the suspicion of broad claims to power, 'imperial' rhetoric of gathering disparate cultures together. Such 'masculine' associations are condemned whomever they cluster around. Even as apparently 'unmasculine' a figure as Ellsworthy can be presented as an outsider coming into the rural community, seeking to control others and referring to the natural world as a 'wench'. Thyrza's claims to sorcery are exposed as sham and Miss Waynflete attacks a young woman with a knife in a parody of a Satanic sacrifice. The novels have more sympathy for the figure of the witch in the landscape, exerting enchantment rather than power, like Bridget. Alison Light and Nicola Humble's account of the 'feminine' turn in literature and culture provides an explanation for how the witchy double vision is deployed and directed: away from power claims and towards enchantment. *Death Comes As the End* provides a dramatic example: a novel set in ancient Egypt, the source of so much symbolism for ritual magic, which presents that symbolism's lack of meaning for a young woman in crisis. Christie's novels do not simply reproduce their sources' views of witchcraft and paganism, but rather engage in the contemporary debate by dramatizing those terms and their implications.

2 Margery Allingham

Margery Allingham's novels rarely focus on witchcraft or paganism, but in three of them – *Look to the Lady* (1931), *Sweet Danger* (1933) and *Cargo of Eagles* (1968, posthumous) – she develops a densely textured vision of an enchanted England. These books combine a strong sense of the magical with an equally insistent system of rational framing and analysis, making them perhaps the strongest examples of the 'double vision' of the witchy detective novel. Allingham presents a landscape which is imbued with traces of earlier customs, inhabited by archetypes who play out earlier patterns of life, but a landscape which is also studied and analysed by academics from outside. The search for folk customs and 'survivals' which Agatha Christie's *Murder Is Easy* presents as a cover story is an animating and enchanting force in these Allingham novels. The books can depict witchcraft beliefs as fulfilling a class-based social function or show a picturesque village as a potential tourist trap, without these dispelling the aura of the supernatural. The rational framework and the feeling of enchantment coexist in Allingham's novels more noticeably than in those of Christie, Ngaio Marsh or Gladys Mitchell. As such they provide a demonstration of one of the central arguments of this Element: that the witchy detective novel developed a mode of fiction which paralleled the mental world of emerging midcentury paganism, holding together the mundane and the supernatural without either cancelling or invalidating the other. In this section I trace the production of this double vision on the levels of themes, events, symbols and even individual sentences. In the conclusion I consider how the novels intersect with the turn to the domestic and how this differs from what was observed in the section on Christie.

   In carrying out a negotiation between the mundane and the supernatural, the novels under discussion draw on a set of theories current in the early twentieth century, which scholars such as Gillian Bennett and Ronald Hutton have labelled 'pagan survivals'. In Hutton's words, this is the influence of nineteenth-century notions of geological change and evolution to human culture: the 'model suggested that the minds of all humans worked in essentially the same way, but had developed at different rates, according to culture and class', and that therefore 'folk customs ... could represent cultural fossils left over from the earlier stages of civilized societies'[78]. This idea had been discredited in archaeology and anthropology by the 1920s, but it remained powerful in folklore circles and became particularly focussed on the idea of such customs as survivals of (and evidence for) pagan beliefs and practices. Tied up with the idealization of the English countryside as an antidote to the forces of modern-ization and industrialization (as described also by Hutton), this became a potent set of assumptions underlying literary and popular visions of the rural world. The deep countryside could be seen as a place in which an earlier, wiser, earthier and more pagan world could still be glimpsed, and where folk customs carried the charge of centuries of pagan belief. The three Allingham novels I discuss engage energetically with the ideas of both 'pagan survivals' and continuity

---

[78] Hutton, *Triumph*, pp. 112–13.

with the English past. They reproduce it, ironize it and critique it, but also use it to frame their sense of England as an enchanted place.

In *Look to the Lady*, Allingham's detective Albert Campion is thrown into a story of a 'lost' heir, an ancestral chalice under threat from a shadowy international gang of crooks and a mysterious apparition in the woods. The Gyrth Chalice at the centre of the novel was entrusted to the Gyrth family centuries before and a legend attached to it claims that if it is taken or lost then the British monarchy will fall. Each heir is initiated into the secrets of the chalice when he comes of age. These facts give a flavour of the 'ritualised feudality' which Susan Rowland identifies in the book.[79]

The novel's air of enchantment is initially constructed via accounts of place and landscape, such as the first description of the area surrounding the Gyrths' ancestral home:

> A little stream ran across the road dividing the two hills; while the cottages, the majority pure Elizabethan, sprawled up each side of the road like sheep asleep in a meadow. It is true that the smithy kept a petrol store housed in a decrepit engine boiler obtained from Heaven knows what dumping ground, but even that had a rustic quality. It was a fairy-tale village peopled by yokels who, if they did not wear the traditional white smocks so beloved of film producers, at least climbed the rough steps to the church on a Sunday morning in top hats of unquestionable antiquity.[80]

Even the description of the place is dialectical, advancing the pastoral image of houses as sheep before admitting the existence of a petrol store and denying that the locals wear smocks before stating that they wear archaic hats on Sundays. Internal space is described with a similar technique when the characters stop at a pub and enter

> the cool brick-floored dining room, which a well-meaning if not particularly erudite management had rendered a little more Jacobean than the Jacobeans. The heavily carved oak beams which supported the ceiling had been varnished to an ebony blackness and the open fireplace at the end of the room was a mass of rusty spits and dogs, in a profusion which would have astonished their original owners.[81]

The pub is authentic and commercialized at the same time: the actual oak beams have been over-varnished to match the popular image of an oak-beamed room, and the genuine antique fire irons are arranged as a signifier of antiquity, though this prevents them from operating as fire irons. The modern use, and the modern

---

[79] Susan Rowland, *From Agatha Christie to Ruth Rendell* (Basingstoke: Palgrave, 2001), p. 127.

[80] Margery Allingham, *Look to the Lady* (London: Jarrolds, 1931, repr. Penguin, 1950), p. 51.

[81] Allingham, *Lady*, p. 43.

way of consuming the past via films or motoring tours, adds an ironic gloss to the genuinely antique elements of the scene, but it does not reveal them to be sham. The hats, the locals and the beams remain genuinely antique and available for the appreciation of the informed eye. Their misappropriation by modern culture guarantees their authenticity, as it shows that the author is not being taken in by a naïve or sentimental idealism. This is a syntactical microcosm of the novel as a whole, which uses characters and episodes in a similar dialectic on a larger scale.

When the topic of witchcraft is introduced in the novel, it is also subject to an ironic scrutiny. Campion's valet Lugg reports having seen a bald woman and having asked the locals about her:

> [A]nd they come out with a yarn about witchcraft and 'aunting and cursin' like a set o' 'eathens. There's too much 'anky-panky about this place. I don't believe in it, but I don't like it. They got a 'aunted wood 'ere … Let's go 'ome.[82]

Campion reacts sceptically, asking if Lugg is 'sure your loquacious friend wasn't a Cook's Guide selling you Rural England, by any chance?'[83] Lugg maintains his dislike of the area and is later found in a hysterical state in a nearby wood at night. He describes being chased by a supernatural creature:

> 'No ordin'ry animal,' said Lugg with decision. 'I'll tell yer what, though,' he conceded, 'it was a like a ten-foot 'igh goat, walkin' on its 'ind legs.'[84]

It transpires that the figure was an elaborate costume worn by the bald woman. She is caught when Campion and an American professor who lives nearby set a trap and catch her. The professor, who has an interest in medieval witchcraft, explains that her activities probably represent a survival of older beliefs. Tellingly, he discusses the matter with Campion in his house with its plaster walls and 'unstained oak beams', suggesting a more realistic approach to the past than the pub.[85]

> It's an example of a blind spot. Modern civilization goes all over the country – all over the world – and yet here and there you come across a patch that hasn't been altered for three hundred years … no doubt at all in my mind that she's descended from a regular line of practising witches. Some of their beliefs have been handed down to her. That costume of hers, for instance, was authentic, and a chant like that is described by several experts. She's a throwback. Probably she realizes what she's doing in only a dim, instinctive sort of fashion. It's most interesting – most interesting.[86]

---

[82] Allingham, *Lady*, p. 64.   [83] Allingham, *Lady*, p. 64.   [84] Allingham, *Lady*, p. 151.
[85] Allingham, *Lady*, p. 155.   [86] Allingham, *Lady*, p. 177.

The theory of survivals is presented here as a reasonable explanation of the apparently supernatural event. It was in one sense a fraud, since there was no nine-foot-high goat creature haunting the wood, but in another sense genuine, since the apparition was the result of very old beliefs manifesting themselves in modern Britain. The professor suggests it represents a more widespread survival of witchcraft in the area:

> 'Of course,' he went on almost hopefully, 'this may have gone on for years. Her mother may have done the same sort of thing . . . after all, if you find these country folk sitting on three hundred year old chairs and using Elizabethan horn spoons to mix their puddings, why shouldn't you find them – very rarely, I admit – practising the black rites of three or four centuries back?[87]

The academic's theory is subtly undermined by one adverb: 'hopefully'. What he offers as a scientific theory is revealed by that term to be an act of faith, proof of his desire to find evidence for what he wishes to exist. Later in the novel, they discover that the woman's activities were not part of a strand of traditional witchcraft, but rather an ad hoc reaction to the family's situation. The old woman and her son with learning difficulties were living on the edge of their community and only survived by poaching in the wood. This happened on the sufferance of other poachers, who would often drive them away, and so the goat costume and chanting provided a useful means of persuading the locals that the wood was dangerously haunted. The professor is forced to revise his theory:

> 'There they were, friendless and practically destitute . . . and there comes to her the memory of what her mother had taught her when she was a girl – all the old beliefs, the peculiar power of the goat. The strange half-forgotten shibboleths come crowding back into her mind, and instinctively she turns it to her own use . . . This isn't the first or last country community that has no sympathy with the weak-minded . . . It's a real primitive story, illustrating, probably, one of the earliest reasons for witchcraft – the terrorization of the strong by the weak. Most interesting.'[88]

Here another level of illusion or sentimentalism is stripped away as we see the dashing of the professor's hopes that he had discovered an unbroken line of witches hidden in the English countryside. He has not found the untouched and pristine rural community with its ancient rituals hidden down the centuries. However, this does not make the witchcraft they have witnessed inauthentic: it is based upon very old materials used by the woman's ancestors and for an authentic purpose. In fact, Campion and the

---

[87] Allingham, *Lady*, p. 178.   [88] Allingham, *Lady*, p. 186.

professor (as well as the unfortunate Lugg) have been present at the rebirth of witchcraft in the village. The same social conditions caused an outcast and destitute woman to carry out the same practices as her forebears, and for the same reasons. In a sense, the story contains something more authentic and ancient than the traces of a fertility rite in a folk dance: it dramatizes the origins of witchcraft themselves coming into effect in the modern age. In a final lively touch of irony, this witch practice is not evidence of the harmony, wisdom and richness of the rural community, as middle-class urban folklorists like the professor were wont to believe. It was the savagery and callousness of a rural community which caused witchcraft to be reborn.

Two years later, Allingham published *Sweet Danger*. In this novel, Campion is tasked by the government with verifying an English family's claim to ancestral lands in Eastern Europe. The lands, suggestively named 'Averna', have suddenly been made strategically significant by an earthquake which created a small deepwater harbour and revealed an oil source in the mountains. The pretext for the adventure story which follows thus combines contemporary geopolitics with historical and mythical associations: the lands were originally granted during a crusade and the mark of sovereignty is a mysterious crown. Indeed, the description of the event which created the harbour teeters between seismology and political metaphor: 'a minor earthquake in the Balkans which shook up Italy and broke some windows in Belgrade'.[89]

This Ruritanian narrative is shaped towards detective fiction by a verbal puzzle. An old manuscript in the British Museum provides an enigmatic description of the coronet which will act as one of the proofs of sovereignty: '*Three drops of blood from a royal wound, three dull stars like a pigeon's egg, held and knit together with a flowery chain. Yet when a Pontisbright do wear it, none shall see it but by the stars.*'[90] The riddle is solved during the course of the novel: the drops and stars are precious stones and when a Pontisbright puts it on, the family's red hair means that the gold and ruby elements fade in comparison to the brightness of the diamonds. The conditions of the riddle's solution are contained in the DNA of the family, associating the rightful heirs physically with the artefacts of the past. A second verbal puzzle is discovered carved into another heirloom, a slice of oak tree:

> 'If Pontisbright would crownéd be,
> Three strange happenings must he see.
> The diamond must be rent in twain
> Before he wear his crown again.

---

[89] Margery Allingham, *Sweet Danger* (London: Heinemann, 1933, repr. Penguin, 1950), p. 29.
[90] Allingham, *Sweet*, p. 39.

Thrice must the mighty bell be toll'd
Before he shall the sceptre hold,
And ere he to his birthright come
Stricken must be Malplaquet drum.'[91]

These conditions are satisfied by pulling apart the necklace to reveal one clue and taking apart a historical drum to reveal another, but the tolling of the bell poses a greater problem. The local church gave up its massive bell to be melted down for munitions during the Zulu War, so its sister bell, now in Switzerland, is broadcast via wireless to a speaker mounted on a local watermill (which has itself been converted to an electricity generator). The resulting enormous sound of a bell tolling from the middle of Europe sets up echoes which rebound from a well in a grove of trees in which the title deeds to the lands are found.

The requirements of the old rhyme are fulfilled, albeit in a way the writer could not have expected or foreseen. The outcome produces the familiar double vision of the enchanted England Allingham depicts: electricity and radio technology resolve the requirements of the riddle, but the outcome is the ratification of an English family's claim to lands awarded to a medieval crusader. The story exists in both the rational and fairy-tale modes. The dialectic between past and present, between authenticity and fakery, seen in *Look to the Lady* is focussed in *Sweet Danger* by the rhyme and the well. Despite being in apparently archaic English, with its use of 'crownéd' and 'stricken', the rhyme mentions the Battle of Malplaquet, dating it to the eighteenth century. The same era is evoked by a telling detail of the well's surroundings: 'As in many meadows that have once been parkland, a fine group of elms stood in the centre, forming a ring round a little depression in the grass.'[92] The implication is that the trees, rather than being a survival of ancient woodland, were in fact planted by eighteenth-century landscaping. Both rhyme and grove are artificial in the sense that they are visibly the product of dateable activity, not relics from the mists of time. Nonetheless, like the varnished beams and superfluous fire-dogs of *Look to the Lady*, these elements take a genuine part in the enchanted England Allingham's work produces. Just as that landscape contained a revival of witchcraft in the earlier novel, in *Sweet Danger*, it contains a revival of wizardry. In keeping with the turn to the domestic and with the attitudes seen in Christie's novels, this activity is corrupt and dangerous. A local doctor is discovered to have been indulging in the more unpleasant reaches of ritual magic, culminating in an attempt to sacrifice several of the heroes in order to raise a demon. He boasts to Campion that the villagers regard him as their Elizabethan ancestors regarded the celebrated magician Dr Dee. The rural landscape provides fertile soil for

---

[91] Allingham, *Sweet*, p. 78.   [92] Allingham, *Sweet*, pp. 219–20.

magical activities to be carried out and for local beliefs to be reawakened, mimicking the patterns of the past. The model established is not one of practices passed down from the immemorial past, but of a context which allows the revival or repetition of magic in atavistic echoes of that past.

At the other end of Allingham's career, *Cargo of Eagles* was left unfinished at her death and was published in 1968 after being completed by her husband, Philip Youngman Carter. Despite this, the text demonstrates continuities with the earlier novels, whether due to elements already in the drafts or because of shared imaginative vision. It creates another enchanted landscape in which the past and present meet, though without such an explicit witchcraft plot. There are strong traces of John Buchan's *Witch Wood* in the opening. It involves Morty, a young half-American academic, being sent to keep an eye on a potentially criminal situation in a village in Essex called Saltey. The narrator notes that 'a great deal about Britain struck him as funny after nearly a year's residence, but he was also deeply attracted by its ancient spell'.[93] The (by now familiar) trope develops of a character entering a rural world in which there are atavistic secrets to be discovered, except that (as with Christie's *Murder Is Easy*) the notion of pagan survivals is the pretext for the visit, not the secret lurking below the surface. Indeed this novel goes a step further: Morty explains to Campion near the beginning of the story that the legend of a local demon 'provides me with a fairly reasonable excuse for hanging around' the village, and he is seen as 'the poor young Yankee professor, good for a free pint and folksy tale any day'.[94] As far as he is concerned, however, the village's claims to atavistic terror are entirely fabricated and the inhabitants merely '[pretend] to be deeply and secretly wicked, which is naive and kind of endearing'.[95] Nonetheless, he mentions that the site's bad reputation 'as a place of ill omen' stretches back to the time of the medieval plague and that 'a peculiarly revolting mother-figure was found in a field at Firestone, four miles away, in nineteen hundred'.[96] The mentions of medieval history, omens and a prehistoric figurine of the kind known as the Willendorf Venus (and supposed to be a fertility goddess) build up around Saltey the cultural and intellectual atmosphere within which folkloric 'survivals' were found and interpreted.

Just as *Look to the Lady* set up a dialectic between complex forms of fraudulence and authenticity, *Cargo of Eagles* suggests that there are genuinely intriguing and strange things in Saltey. Campion and Morty's conversation provides the local inn as an example:

---

[93] Margery Allingham, *Cargo of Eagles* (London: Chatto and Windus, 1968, repr., undated) e-book loc. 32.

[94] Allingham, *Cargo*, loc. 145.   [95] Allingham, *Cargo*, loc. 16.

[96] Allingham, *Cargo*, loc. 109.

'I didn't know he was at the inn. Did you say it was called The Demon?'

' ... It used to be called The Foliage, which she was mistaken enough to think dull.' Morty met the other man's raised eyebrows and laughed. 'I know. It can only be a contraction of "The Foliate Man", can't it? I tell you the place is full of good things. Add that to the Fertility Venus and one or two other items, and the shenanigans the wilder teen-age gangs get up to along the sea wall don't seem half as modern as they might.'[97]

Renaming the inn 'The Demon' is explained as part of the village's attempt to present a sinister olde-worlde atmosphere and attract the tourist trade, but in doing so they obscure a genuine survival of an older past, the 'Green Man' widely regarded as a folkloric trace of pagan gods. Rather like the over-varnished beams in the pub in *Look to the Lady*, 'The Demon' is both an attempt to commercialize an imaginary past and an authentically old artefact underneath the gloss. Despite Morty's sophisticated scorn for the villagers' pretence of rural wickedness, he is still drawn in to believe that there is something atavistic about the life of Saltey. He connects the 'mother-figure' (now retitled a 'Fertility Venus') with the activities of the teenaged gangs, implying that the modern motorbike riders are instinctively enacting a form of fertility rite or sex magic. The distinctions between the past and the present are breaking down as before, even if not in the ways commercial consumption of the past would dictate. An additional layer of irony is provided by the fact that it is Morty's multiple degrees and middle-class intellectualism which make him believe in this enchanted landscape. Without it, he would see only an ugly figurine and some teenaged hoodlums, but as a folklore enthusiast and scholar he sees the 'ancient spell' of Britain.

The dialectic continues to develop around the pub when, on the first occasion Morty meets the landlord of the Demon (formerly the Foliage), the latter quotes a line of poetry: 'To the world's end have I come. To the world's end.'[98] Morty correctly identifies it as a quotation from the libretto of *The Immortal Hour*, an Edwardian opera about characters crossing over from the human world to the supernatural realm. As the landlord remarks, the words are by the poet William Sharp, published under the pseudonym 'Flora Macleod'. Sharp was a late nineteenth- and early twentieth-century man of letters whose career as a writer under his own name foundered with his launch of *The Pagan Review* in 1892. It recovered when he invented a Celtic twilight alter ego named Flora Macleod and published works under her name. As a literary allusion this adds to the sceptical ironic portrayal of Saltey by reminding the alert reader of both the Victorian-Edwardian thirst for rural paganism and the near-fraudulent forms in which that desire could manifest itself.

---

[97] Allingham, *Cargo*, loc. 157.   [98] Allingham, *Cargo*, loc. 1029.

As the chaos typical of an Allingham novel develops, the pub becomes the centre of an invasion of the bikers, as described by Lugg:

> 'And that's another item which is not the article, if you take me. Very mackaber. Ton-up kids wearing voodoo masks. They're 'orrible enough themselves, without that.'
>
>   'Masks?' inquired Mr Campion mildly. 'Did you say voodoo masks?'
>
>   'That's exackly what I said.' Mr Lugg was truculent. 'Like those shrunken heads which are just the job for making the parlor look 'omely when you come back from a luxury cruise to central Africa.'[99]

As soon as the bikers' masks are mentioned here, they are framed in terms of commerce and authenticity with the reference to 'shrunken heads' as interior decor and as signalling luxury travel to exotic locations. The echoes of *Witch Wood* also become stronger at this point with its group of atavistic figures engaged in the 'pagan' activities of sex and violence, masked like the cultists in Buchan's novel.

At the novel's climax, a stash of gold is discovered which was stolen from a boat during the Second World War, incidentally revealing the meaning of the title *Cargo of Eagles*. In Campion's words, they are: 'Double Eagles … Twenty-dollar gold pieces. Pirate gold – fairy gold – a king's ransom. It depends how you look at them.'[100] In this denouement, the novel's multiple vision becomes explicit. The money can exist in both the mythical mode and the realist one. The use for which Campion intends the gold also has two potential aspects. On a literal level, instead of returning it to the government department which issued it, he intends to use it to fund the escape of a female intelligence agent captured on the other side of the Iron Curtain. On a mythical level, given the 'mystical royalism' which Rowland has identified in Allingham's work, it can be read as analogous to Drake's or Raleigh's escapades, a modern act of privateering.

Conclusion

These novels exemplify the double vision of the midcentury witchy detective novel, meticulously constructing a textual matrix within which the landscape can be both modern and enchanted. Allingham regularly invokes the notion of pagan survivals and engages it in a dialectic technique which renders it inhabitable during the fiction, if not plausible on its own terms. As I have suggested, she offers a vision of rural England in which a country pub can be both a tourist trap and a genuinely archaic artefact. The witch of *Look to the Lady* and the bikers of *Cargo of Eagles* are presented as spontaneous and authentic

---

[99] Allingham, *Cargo*, loc. 2351.   [100] Allingham, *Cargo*, loc. 3169.

recreations of ancient ways of being, though those ways are less charming and more earthy than the popular folklore of the time would suggest. They are survivals which result not from a long and attenuated tradition being passed down, but rather from the same past conditions pressing upon modern humans, who use the material around them to instinctively re-enact their ancestors' activities. The two American professors provide an outside perspective, allowing Allingham to present her magical England as seen through a supposedly objective intellectual lens, but even they are subject to irony and relativization. Their folkloric enthusiasm demonstrates their infatuation with their own theories about the ancient survivals in the rural social milieu, and those theories are proved right in ways which they did not predict.

The professors with their interest in the history and culture of rural England also highlight these novels' engagement with the turn to the domestic. All three books are intrigued by the possibilities of turning inwards into the depths of England and the American characters contribute to this movement. The grail quest of *Look to the Lady* pits an anonymous and vague international cartel against the closely textured world of the Gyrths, with the latter getting the better of the comparison. Unlike the Christie novels examined previously, however, these texts are more comfortable with the rural depths being connected to worlds outside. After all, the hunt for heirlooms in *Sweet Danger* is intended to allow the newly revealed deepwater harbour and oil reserves of Avernus to come within the ambit of British foreign policy. This looks surprisingly like the kind of imperial adventuring which Alison Light describes British literature and culture as eschewing in the interwar years. However, it is still explicable within the turn to the domestic, though via a different route, since the novel's action takes place entirely within enchanted England. The solution to the sudden crisis, which shook Italy and broke windows in Belgrade, is to be found in the depths of the English rural landscape: the 'domestic' is the answer even to overseas problems. This becomes even more evident in the denouement of *Cargo of Eagles*, when the reader discovers both the nature of the treasure and the reason Campion wants to secure it. The secrets of Saltey, where paganism and atavism run riot, are to be spent in an unofficial deal to repatriate a female agent captured during a Cold War intrigue. Her imagined return is a powerful image of the turn to the domestic.

3 Ngaio Marsh

Ngaio Marsh's novels demonstrate a resolute scepticism towards esoteric, syncretic and occult religious ideas. Where witchcraft is mentioned in her work, it tends to be framed within this constellation of disapproval. At the same time, the books demonstrate an interest in what may lie behind such religious ideas, offering a sense of something mysterious, powerful and dangerous to articulate. As soon as magic takes an external or organized form in Marsh's novels, it is criticized. Magical and esoteric practices are shown as cover stories, metaphors or logical extensions of sinister forces in the mundane world such as drug addiction, swindling, men's domination of women and illicit forms of sex. In this she demonstrates an extreme version of one of the elements identifiable elsewhere in the witchy detective novel: a suspicion of magic as a set of claims to power. Nonetheless, she constructs her own version of the enchanted double vision, though in a less explicit way. Her settings admit the possibility of the non-rational, though they dramatize the dangers of articulating it. This tendency in her novels can be understood within the turn to the domestic I have been tracing through previous sections. Marsh's narratives demonstrate a suspicion of the syncretism which ritual magic can involve, including its claims to synthesize and bring under control widely spread historical and cultural material. This suspicion is recognizable as the discomfort with imperialist rhetoric which Alison Light identifies in the midcentury novel, transposed into a supernatural key. It is strongest in *Death in Ecstasy* (1936) and *Spinsters in Jeopardy* (1954). The same turn to the domestic can be recognized in the rural English settings of the two Marsh novels in which enchantment appears to be possible: *Off with His* Head (1957) and *Dead Water* (1963). *When in Rome* (1970) hints at the creative power of the pagan past but also warns against trying to exploit it.

Death in Ecstasy involves a murder which takes place during the rites of a small syncretic religious group in London, the 'House of the Sacred Flame'. The narrative owes something to the public scandal over the 'Temple of Truth' cult in New Zealand, but its fictional form recalls a recent fantastical bestseller, Dennis Wheatley's *The Devil Rides Out* (1934), which had introduced the wider public to images of cultic depravity and mortal peril. The identity of the murderer is less vivid in *Death in Ecstasy* than the depiction of the unwholesome and exploitative 'House' presided over by the sinister Father Jasper Garnette. It is clear from both the narrative voice and Inspector Alleyn's that the reader should not take the group's spiritual potential seriously: the first page refers suavely to how 'all sorts of queer religions squeak, like mice in the wainscoting', behind the 'tedious façade' of a London Sunday.[101] The last chapter mentions the likelihood that now the 'Sacred Flame' has closed down, another 'side-show for the credulous' will spring up in its place.[102]

---

[101] Ngaio Marsh, *Death in Ecstasy* (London: Geoffrey Bles, 1936, repr. HarperCollins, 2009), p. 9.
[102] Marsh, *Ecstasy*, p. 250.

The ceremonies of the 'House' are elaborately syncretic, with statues of a range of pagan deities, a faux communion rite and sermons in which Fr Garnette hypnotizes his listeners. During the investigation, this unappealing religious decoration is shown to obscure various forms of corruption and exploitation: fleecing congregation members, dealing drugs and seducing female worshippers. The murder which begins the novel is revealed to be the result of the various interwoven strands of intrigue and corruption which centred on the 'House': it is the outcome of human selfishness, greed and weakness being indulged and given ritual form by the rites of the Sacred Flame. In the moral vision of this novel, the pseudo-religion provides not only an incense screen to obscure simpler and base motives, but a way for those motives to ramify into murder.

The same constellation of ritual magic, drugs, sexual exploitation and self-deceit can be observed two decades later in *Spinsters in Jeopardy*. The plotting and narrative of this novel resemble a thriller more than a detective novel, with relatively little ratiocination and instead a series of events which bring the reader closer and closer to the centre of a cult. The kinds of magical practice indulged in by the group and the history they represent are explicitly condemned and scorned by Alleyn in a lengthy passage of reflection:

> He turned over in his mind all he had read of that curious expression of human credulity called magic … its witness to man's industry in pursuit of a chimera. Hundreds and hundreds of otherwise intelligent men, he found, had subjected themselves throughout the centuries to the boredom of memorising and reciting senseless formulae, to the indignity of unspeakable practices and to the threat of the most ghastly reprisals.[103]

He goes on to consider how both the practice and the punishment attached to magic involved hardship, including starvation, fear, torture and burning, 'and all without any first hand evidence of the smallest success'.[104] Many of the magicians 'ended by falling into their own traps', as 'the hysteria they induced was refracted upon them' and in 'the reek of the ceremonial smoke they too began to look for the terrifying reward'.[105] Here is a more explicit account of the irony I identified in *Death in Ecstasy*: the cultic practices may operate as a cover for base and comprehensible desires for power, sex and money, but they end up producing more terrible effects than those desires on their own.

In these two novels, the mysteries are fraudulent and it is the act of making them into rites and texts which creates their effects. In later books, the mysteries are apparently more real, though still dangerous to articulate. This issue of

---

[103] Ngaio Marsh, *Spinsters in Jeopardy* (London: William Collins, 154, repr. Fontana, 1986), p.223.
[104] Marsh, *Spinsters*, p. 223. [105] Marsh, *Spinsters*, p. 223.

articulation runs as a theme through the reactions of various characters to the occult. The priests and magicians themselves are fond of glib flows of symbolic speech. Their adherents occasionally produce the same effect by the derangement of normal typography. The doorkeeper at the House of the Sacred Flame declares that the voice they can hear is 'an Invocation' and excuses himself from further speech by stating, 'It is against our Rule for me to gossip while I am On Guard,' whilst the narrator comments that he 'seemed to speak in capitals'.[106] The same joke appears when Troy first speaks to one of the spinsters of the other novel's title, who asks her, 'Are you interested in The Truth?', whilst the narrator notes that 'Troy was too addled with unseasonable sleep and a surfeit of anxiety to hear the capital letters.'[107] The trope combines a level of intellectual (and social) snobbery with the theme of language straining to contain something beyond its normal range of reference. Another form of misarticulation appears in the emotional, working-class spirituality of characters Alleyn encounters in the novels. In *Death in Ecstasy*, the victim's old nanny is appalled both at her death and at the state of spiritual peril which surrounds it:

> 'The sight of the place, full of naked heathen idols and all the baubles of Satan – it was worse than Rome. There! And when I found out she was going to be the leader in that lewd mockery of her own Church I wished she had died when she was an innocent baby.'[108]

Alleyn and his friend Nigel recognize in this tirade the non-Conformist tradition, labelling it 'real revivalist fervour, pig-headed, stupid, arrogant' (and, in comparison with the House of the Sacred Flame, 'blessedly straightforward and clean').[109] Nanny's equivalent in the southern French milieu of *Spinsters in Jeopardy* is another working-class woman, Teresa. Her religion is carried on at an equally high emotional temperature, though in a different confessional orientation, with phrases such as 'The Holy Virgin is my witness' and 'I am under the protection of Our Lady of Paysdoux for whom I have a special devotion.'[110]

Though both Nanny and Teresa's religious outbursts appear more attractive than the mucky syncretism of the cults, and suitable to their backgrounds, they are presented as far from the detective's or (implicitly) the reader's experience. The speeches of these two 'character turns' are themselves misarticulations of mystery, even if more time-honoured ones. Only Marsh's detective is shown as suitably reticent in the face of the potentially supernatural. In *Spinsters in Jeopardy*, Alleyn undergoes a brief moment of dislocation, roughly corresponding to an 'out of body experience'. The passage is worth quoting at length:

[106] Marsh, *Ecstasy*, p. 14.   [107] Marsh, *Ecstasy*, p. 53.   [108] Marsh, *Ecstasy*, p. 129.
[109] Marsh, *Ecstasy*, p. 129.   [110] Marsh, *Spinsters*, pp. 161, 162.

He sat on the bed staring into the dark and thinking of the events of the long day and of Troy and Ricky and presently a familiar experience revisited him. He seemed to see himself for the first time, a stranger, a being divorced from experience, a chrysalis from which his spirit had escaped and which it now looked upon, he thought, with astonishment as a soul might look after death at its late housing. He thought: 'I suppose Oberon imagines he's got all this sort of thing taped. Raoul and Teresa too, after their fashion and belief. But I have never found an answer.' The illusion, if it was an illusion and he was never certain about this, could be dismissed, but he held to it still and in a little while he found he was looking at a fluorescence, a glimmering of something, no more than a bat-light. It grew into a shape. It was Ricky's little figurine faithfully illuminating itself in the dark. And Ricky's voice still rather fretful, brought Alleyn back to himself.

'Daddy!' he was shouting, 'is he doing it? Daddy!'[111]

Alleyn's personal spiritual experiences appear to be set as a counterpoint to the florid and dangerous outward expressions of spiritual self-indulgence seen in *Overture to Death* and more particularly here in *Spinsters in Jeopardy*. Marsh balances the language of spiritual transcendence, 'a chrysalis from which his spirit had escaped ... as a soul might look ... at its late housing', with the language of scepticism, 'I have never found an answer ... the illusion, if it was an illusion'. The feeling is then integrated back into the novel's mundane world in ways which only raise more questions. Alleyn sees a light, a symbol of transcendence, but it turns out to his son's toy goat which glows in the dark, and he hears him asking, 'Is he doing it?' This can be read as a debunking of the pseudo-religious nonsense which has been so lethal during the novel. Alternatively, Alleyn's transcendent experience can be read as showing for a second that the objects of the mundane world – a light, the figure of a goat, a voice calling to him – do hold some mysterious greater significance. This is further suggested by Alleyn's reflection that Oberon, the cult leader, 'imagines he's got all this sort of thing taped'. His instinctive criticism of Oberon is not that he would blow the moment out of all proportion, but that he would provide too neat and simple an account of it, reducing its real significance. The passage insists on the mysterious quality of Alleyn's experience, refusing to either codify it or dismiss it. The moment combines two elements typical of the witchy detective novel: an enchanted double vision and a scepticism about organized magic. The proportions here are very different from other novels I have mentioned. *Murder Is Easy* and *Sweet Danger*, for example, focus most of their supernatural attention on the enchanted double vision of a world which could be interpreted in mundane or in magical ways. The sinister figures of male

---

[111] Marsh, *Spinsters*, pp. 182–3.

magicians, which contrast with the enchantment of the setting, are relatively minor subplots. In Marsh's novel, the proportions are reversed, with an entire narrative of cultic magic and only a fleeting experience of enchantment. Nonetheless, the elements are visible here and, in Marsh's next pagan novels, the feeling of enchantment is more prominent.

Off with His Head (1957) and *Dead Water* (1964) develop both the sense of the supernatural and the theme that it is dangerous to articulate mysteries. Both depict small communities in which something remarkable or uncanny happens. The former involves a rural village with a traditional annual dance believed to go back for many centuries, the latter a seaside village in which a young boy is apparently miraculously cured of disfiguring warts by washing his hands in a spring. In both novels, a murder takes place in the swirl of events surrounding the uncanny element. The murder at the centre of *Off with His Head* takes place at the climax of a ritual folk dance held around a dolmen in a rural village during the winter solstice. As this summary might imply, it is more engaged than any of Marsh's other novels with ideas of folklore and rural paganism. These ideas are mainly mediated to the audience through three main characters: the visiting folklore enthusiast Anna Bünz, the local medical man Dr Otterley and the detective Roderick Alleyn. The former is a generally comic figure, mentioned by Hutton as one of a series of recognizable figures in the fiction of the mid twentieth century: the maiden lady folklorist.[112] She is given to the kind of coy archaism which E. F. Benson satirized gently in his Riseholme novels, signalled in lines such as:

> "'St Agnes Eve, ach bitter chill it was!'" . . . 'But I see no sign,' she added to herself, 'of hare nor owl, nor of any living creature, godamercy.' She was pleased with this improvisation. Her intimate circle had lately adopted 'god-amercy' as an amusing expletive.[113]

On the same page, she is described as humming the song known as 'Sellinger's Round', though the narrative adds '(from her Playford album)'.[114] This ensures the reader appreciates that her knowledge of English folk culture comes from anthologies and collections, or is at least filtered through those lenses when she encounters it in the rural wild. The doctor maintains rather more English irony about his enthusiasm for folklore, but is convinced that the local dance is something ancient and deeply significant. This can be seen in a remarkable and lengthy exchange with Alleyn, which is revealing of both men. The doctor

---

[112] Hutton, *Triumph*, p. 128.
[113] Ngaio Marsh, *Off with His Head* (London: William Collins, 1957, repr. HarperCollins, 2009) e-book loc. 70.
[114] Marsh, *Head*, loc. 77.

refers to his interests as a 'hobby-horse', which leads him on an excursus on 'how many everyday phrases derive from the folk-drama' including 'Horseplay! Playing the fool! Cutting capers! Midsummer madness!' and the pub name 'the Green Man'. Picking up his cue, Alleyn asks if the 'concept of the ritual dance' originates in 'Frazer's King of the Sacred Grove' and enacts a 'fertility rite-cum-sacrifice-death-and-resurrection', to which Otterley agrees, calling it 'the oldest manifestation of the urge to survive and the belief in redemption through sacrifice and resurrection'. His account of the cultural connections within this network of symbolism includes references to specific other folk dances, and calls it 'as its lowest, a few scraps of half-remembered jargon', and when he suggests it has a higher form, Alleyn suggests, 'Not – by any chance – Lear?'[115] As this passage shows, Alleyn is demonstrably well possessed of the cultural touchstones which enable him to make sense of the doctor's theories. He may not be enthusiastic about folklore and pagan survivals himself, but he is familiar with classical literature, the theories Frazer expounded in *The Golden Bough*, and the parallels to be drawn between high art and folk culture. The novel stops short of exactly endorsing or debunking the folkloric swirl of ideas so enthusiastically pursued by Anna Bünz and expounded by Dr Otterley, but they are treated with much greater respect and indulgence than the esoteric cults of *Death in Ecstasy* and *Spinsters in Jeopardy*. The depiction of a rich and complex rural world, complete with customs and traces of older ways of life, approaches those provided by Allingham.

The plot, as it develops, certainly suggests that there is something mysterious about the Dance of the Five Sons. The murder takes place during the dance and can be causally linked to Bünz's obsessive interest in folklore. One of the dancers is a local misfit named Simon Begg. A grocer's son who now runs a garage, he has long wished to turn the local smithy into a petrol station, but the old smith refuses to sell. With the arrival of Bünz, Begg sees an opportunity to make some cash, offering to let her get even closer to the folk dance than simply watching it. For a price, Begg swaps her into his costume, allowing her to actually participate in the supposedly ancient ritual and to perhaps even hear the secret words whispered at the climax of the dance. Whilst everyone supposes he is in the dancing costume, Begg sees a momentary opportunity to kill the old smith and does so, removing the only obstacle to his taking over the smithy. His act of trading money for his place in the solstice dance represents his inability to take the place offered him in the society and culture where he grew up. Instead he took a chance to turn the local culture into a commodity experience. However, it was only Bünz's willingness to pay for the chance to be in the

---

[115] Marsh, *Head*, loc. 2173.

dance which meant that Begg was present and unseen when a chance to kill the old smith appeared. He had not planned to do so. Thus the novel's plotting connects the desire to 'collect' folklore traditions and the willingness to sell them with the killing. Unlike the cults of *Ecstasy* or *Spinsters*, the (supposedly) pagan dance of *Off with His Head* does not seem to be lethal in itself. It does not indulge human vices which can be nurtured into violence. Rather, the incursion and prying into that folkloric world from outside, enabled by one of its members, unleashes a series of chances which lead to the murder. There is a genuine sense that the rural milieu contains a powerful mystery, though not one that can be explained or accounted for. Just as Alleyn's out-of-body experience in *Spinsters* resists articulation, the solstice dance resists attempts to do the same. At the centre of dance is the moment when the old smith pokes his head through an interlaced ring of five mock swords and mutters some traditional words which go with his role. The attempt by Bünz to discover and record those words leads to tragedy. In *Off with His Head*, Marsh presents the reader with a more developed symbol of a mystery which cannot be articulated or handled without becoming corrupt and even dangerous.

Dead Water depicts another small community, this time a seaside village in the West Country. Walter Trehern, a local boy with learning disabilities, has an odd experience at a rock pool by a spring. He seems to see a lady in green who tells him to wash his hands, which are afflicted with warts. He does so, and the next morning the warts have fallen off. The story spreads and prompts interest both from people hoping for similarly miraculous 'cures' and from those intrigued by the supernatural. Some of those who visit the spring report improvements in their medical conditions. The local area benefits from the increased tourism and the spring is put behind a toll gate. A festival is planned to celebrate the spring. Walter becomes something of a local celebrity and his parents encourage him to ask for tips from the tourists. The kind of commercialization which happened only on a small scale (though with large consequences) in *Off with His Head* becomes a major theme of the novel and poses a moral dilemma. This theme comes into sharp relief as an impromptu meeting of the town establishment is held in the local pub. Two years have passed and the ownership of the land which includes the spring has been inherited by someone else, who regards the whole matter as nonsense. They have given instructions to take down the toll gate and disclaim all the supposed cures. As the festival is threatened with cancellation and the spring with being opened to the public without charge, the mayor is worried about the village's new-found prosperity ebbing away. He addresses the rector, suggesting that his studied neutrality on the question of the potentially 'miraculous' cures is not disinterested and asking, 'what you reckon would have happened to your Church Restoration

Fund if Portcarrow hadn't benefited by the Spring to the extent it has done?'[116] The rector embarrassedly agrees that no such money would have been available. A similar exchange takes place with the doctor, who insists that 'I . . . haven't disguised my views. I have an open mind about these cases. I have neither encouraged nor discouraged my patients to make use of the Spring.'[117] Another member of the meeting retorts that 'from that impregnable position . . . you've added a dozen rooms to your bloody nursing home'. Studied disinterest has the effect of collusion with the feverish interest of both locals and tourists in the medicinal powers of the spring water and the patronage of the green lady. The boy whose warts disappeared is already being exploited in at least two ways – being offered by his parents as a tourist attraction to the visitors and by the local folklore enthusiasts as the centrepiece of their folk festival.

Once again, the motif of inarticulability emerges from the foolishness, the greed and the genuine uncertainty of the novel. The opening chapter narrates the vision at the spring from the boy's point of view, leaving the reader with the possibility of believing that he imagined it and his warts healed themselves by natural processes (such as washing in icy water), that something genuinely supernatural occurred, or that some combination of the two resulted in the story he told. The boy's learning disabilities mean he is not able to explain exactly what happened; or, rather, the locals are not able to extract the kind of information they would find valuable from his account of the experience. It is certain that he underwent an experience which he found mysterious and moving and which had an effect on him. The results of him sharing that experience with others are disastrous. His vision is co-opted and exploited by others, however high-minded their intentions might be. *Dead Water* presents Marsh's recurrent motif of a nebulous and mysterious *something* which cannot be articulated without the risk of exploitation and corruption. Walter's silence at the spring joins Alleyn's sight of his own body and the Old Guiser's muttering in the ring of swords. The book's very refusal to articulate whatever mystery happens in these moments contributes to Marsh's version of the witchy double vision. The reader is left able to decide whether to interpret these events within a rational or a supernatural framework. The thicker description of the settings in these two books, combined with the more sympathetic characters surrounding the uncanny events, nudges the emotional tone towards the possibility of non-rational readings.

When in Rome (1970) develops most fully these two central aspects of Marsh's presentation of paganism: the feeling of ancient mystery and the

---

[116] Ngaio Marsh, *Dead Water* (London: William Collins, 1964, repr. Fontana, 1983), p. 45.

[117] Marsh, *Water*, p. 45.

dangers posed by crass or hasty articulation of the content of the mysterious. The plot centres on Barnaby Grant, a novelist who is conducting a party of sightseers around Rome, focussing on places featured in his famous novel *Simon in Latium*. The book was inspired by his experience of exploring San Tommaso, a Roman church which has an older Christian structure below it and an even more ancient temple to Mithras on the bottom level. *When in Rome* offers this as a symbol of creative mystery, reaching down into the depths below modern culture to the atavistic spaces and symbols which underlie the activity above. The fact that it is never quite explained what about the site sparked Grant's imagination adds to the sense that such experiences cannot be pinpointed or analysed. Grant finds his role as tour guide particularly distasteful and is only carrying it out because he is being blackmailed by Sebastian Mailer. Mailer trapped Grant with an elaborate scam which meant that when *Simon in Latium* was published, Mailer possessed a novella which Grant appeared to have plagiarized. Grant had previously been suspected of plagiarism over an earlier novel (though Marsh makes clear this was a creative coincidence), and so was sufficiently worried about Mailer's threat to reveal the supposed source of his book that he took on the tour as a celebrity guide. I have given this account of the pre-plot of the book, which is revealed during the narrative of *When in Rome*, because it emphasizes certain themes of Marsh's novel. Almost everything that Marsh feels is worthy and valuable in this novel – Grant's first visit to Rome, the inspiration which the sites there gave him, the artistic creation of his book – has already happened before the novel itself starts. The events that we witness during the narrative are a revisiting of the Rome which inspired Grant, the reading from his book which he reluctantly gives is a rerunning of the moment of creativity he experienced, and it is undertaken to protect *Simon in Latium* from an accusation that it is itself a rehashing of someone else's work. In doing so, Grant's creative originality becomes packaged and sold as a commercial product which others can experience in a second-hand recreation. *When in Rome*'s insistence on inspiration and creativity as singular and unrepeatable experiences, articulable only in the art form which they give rise to (rather than as commentary or franchising), develops the theme of the inarticulable quality of the mysterious.

The pagan elements are intertwined with this theme of creativity and hidden meaning. A well plumbs the depths through the layers, providing an apt symbol for the descent the tourists make into the remains of the past. The layers of pagan and Christian material, though depicted here in Rome and in terms of architecture, strike a familiar note from novels like *Off with His Head* and *Cargo of Eagles*. It literalizes the notion of ancient pagan elements submerged beneath modern life and accessible via some form of excavation or subterranean journeying down through that surface. This sense of pagan and Christian occupying the same space, alongside the insistence that great circumspection is necessary in articulating mystery (even to the point of silence), is caught by a passage in which Grant conducts the party through the church above the Mithraic temple:

> She herself was caught up in wonder at the great golden bowl-shaped mosaic of the apse. Acanthus and vine twisted tenderly together to enclose little groups of everyday persons going about their medieval business. The Cross, dominant though it was, seemed to have grown out of some pre-Christian tree. 'I shall say nothing about the apse,' Grant said. 'It speaks for itself.'[118]

When they reach the lower levels, he is persuaded to read a passage from *Simon in Latium* in which the hero stands in the same spot and feels he is mystically in touch with the past. Unbeknownst to the characters at the time (including Grant), this is the moment when one of them slips away to commit the murder.

> He read rapidly and badly in an uninflected voice but something of the character of his writing survived the treatment.
> ' – Nothing had changed. The dumpy god with Phrygian cap, icing-sugar ringlets, broken arms and phallus rose with his matrix of stony female breasts. A rather plebeian god one might have said, but in his presence fat little Simon's ears heaved with the soundless roar of a sacrificial bull, his throat and the back of his nose were stung by blood that nineteen centuries ago had boiled over white-hot stone, and his eyes watered in the reek of burning entrails. He trembled and was immeasurably gratified.'[119]

Even with Grant reading out his own work verbatim the passage suggests that a derivative and second-hand action is taking place, with only 'something of the character of the writing' remaining for the audience to grasp.[120] The suspicion of mediation and articulation of the mysterious which runs through Marsh's novels extends even to a novelist's mediation of his own book. It certainly condemns a return to the site of artistic inspiration in order to turn the scene into a tourist attraction. That site, moreover, involves a well shaft running through the archaeological layers, producing another mystical void equivalent to the ring of swords in *Off with His Head* or the pool in *Dead Water*. Whatever experience Grant had in that void becomes tarnished and even risky when it is exposed to comment and commercialization.

The murder itself takes place when one of the tourists, a Dutch publisher who is also being blackmailed by Mailer, kills him in order to prevent the discovery of his secret. His marriage involves an unspecified degree of incest: whether his

---

[118] Ngaio Marsh, *When in Rome* (London: William Collins, 1970, repr. Fontana, 1971), p. 54.

[119] Marsh, *Rome*, p. 70.   [120] Marsh, *Rome*, p. 70.

wife is his stepsister or half-sister is not entirely clear. Either way, it would be enough to ruin the man, who runs a Puritanical family publishing firm. Throughout the novel this couple (named Van der Veydel) are compared to a funerary sculpture of an Etruscan bride and bridegroom which Grant sees in the Villa Giulia at the opening of the story. He is struck by their enigmatic smiles and the similarity of their features and, when he meets the Van der Veydels, he mentally refers to them as the 'Etruscans'. An Etruscan sculpture alongside Roman artefacts in a Renaissance papal palace provides a similar layering of historical traces as the church of San Tommaso. During a conversation at the end of the novel, when Alleyn reveals that he knows that Van der Veydel committed the murder, the latter claims that his family stretches back to the time of the Etruscans: 'I may tell you that I believe our family, which is of great antiquity, arose in classical times in the lands between the Tiber and the Arno.'[121] Alleyn does not denounce him publicly and expresses sympathy both for his love for his wife and for his predicament in being blackmailed. The novel's condemnation is reserved for Mailer's manipulation and dishonesty. When read through the patterns visible in the Marsh novels discussed earlier, Mailer's death happened at the confluence of two actions: firstly, his coercing of Grant to return to the well down the centuries at San Tommaso, in order to cheapen the inspiration which gave rise to *Simon in Latium*; secondly, his blackmailing of Van der Veydel at the same site, where they were in the presence of the ancient past. Tampering with and attempting to exploit the mysterious has led to Mailer's death, and Marsh's book seems to consider this justice enough.

Conclusion

March's novels cannot be said to present an appealing picture of witchcraft and paganism, at least as a religious system or syncretic practice. As I have discussed, *Death in Ecstasy* and *Spinsters in Jeopardy* reverse the proportions of enchantment and warning found in novels such as *Sweet Danger* or *Murder Is Easy*. The unpleasant ritual magicians provide the overwhelming proportion of the narrative in comparison to a fleeting suggestion of the numinous. The latter can barely be described within novels which are so suspicious of magical texts. Even the uncanny elements in the more sympathetically portrayed settings of *Dead Water* and *Off with His Head* lead to disaster and death when they are explored or exploited by the locals. However, the mysterious elements are not subjected to the kind of debunking which takes place in *The Pale Horse* or Gladys Mitchell's *Nest of Vipers* (which I discuss in the next section).

---

[121] Marsh, *Rome*, p. 218.

The process of exposing fraud and exploitation reveals the venerable traditions of human credulity and greed for power which attract people to magical practices. This resolute scepticism about ritual magic becomes comprehensible when placed alongside the other witchy detective novels discussed in this Element. It is part of the turn to the domestic, rejecting a syncretic, expansive and even 'imperialistic' rhetoric of power in favour of an enchantment rooted in the landscape and the culture.

This enchantment produces a version of the double vision familiar from other sections, though more fleeting and elusive. The narrative does not insist that the reader accept the existence of supernatural elements in the fictional world, but neither are they exposed. It is perfectly possible to read *Off with His Head* or *When in Rome* as books about people who believe untrue things about the likelihood of being in touch with ancient and mysterious sources of inspiration. However, the tone and atmosphere of these novels add weight to at least indulging that possibility, if only because more of the text becomes meaningful if it is read in that way. In the case of *When in Rome*, the novel's apparently anomalous ending makes more sense if the reader gives weight to the mysterious elements in the book. Sebastian Mailer's death looks more merited, and Alleyn's covering up for the criminal more justified, if the blackmailer was tampering with ancient sources of inspiration. Paradoxically, a non-rational reading offers a more cohesive pattern of reason in this case. From the unpleasant ritual exploitation of *Death in Ecstasy* and *Spinsters in Jeopardy*, through the rural ambiguity of *Off with His Head* and *Dead Water*, to the well into the past of *When in Rome*, Marsh's novels progressively develop this sense of the mysterious and inarticulable which holds creative and inspiring possibilities, but which can all too easily become corrupted and dangerous.

4 Gladys Mitchell

Mrs Beatrice Adela Lestrange Bradley, Gladys Mitchell's detective, is continually described as witchlike. She cackles, she disconcerts people with her knowledge of the occult arts, and she displays preternatural insight into their thoughts. At rare moments, she even performs, or appears to perform, witchcraft and ritual magic. However, it is not always when Mitchell is describing her detective's beaky nose or cackling laugh that the stories engage most strongly with the characteristic modes of the witchy detective novel. These moments signal the books' interest in magic and witchcraft, but it is in the movements of characters through the English landscape that Mitchell constructs an enchanted double vision. The acts of disrupting the normal unreflective relationship with the land by floating through it, or running over it, or even digging down into it, provide moments of transformation for characters who find themselves playing mythical or magical roles. This demonstrates the powerful influence of the turn to the domestic. The inward move Alison Light identified as a form of mid-century resistance to internationalist and imperial concerns becomes literalized in these characters' engagement with the landscape. They are placed amidst or within it, presented as part of its enchantments. The double vision this establishes in Mitchell's novels can also involve what Marion Gibson has punningly described as a witch's power of 'bi-location', a concept covering both the occupying of multiple spaces and lesbian subtext. Gibson borrows the version of the term from Jane Garrity's discussion of Sylvia Townsend Warner's *Lolly Willowes* and it is useful for recognizing the potential for witch narratives in Mitchell's novels to acknowledge relationships between women which include solidarity, passionate affection and sexual attraction.[122] I trace the development of these elements in Mitchell's work from the late 1930s, when they begin to appear in *Come Away, Death*, until the late 1970s, when *Nest of Vipers* presents them in a disenchanted mode.

In *Come Away, Death* (1937), the English landscape is itself the uncanny double of the spaces the characters move through. The novel recounts an expedition to Greece by an eccentric Classicist, Sir Rudri Hopkinson. The trip is taken in order to recreate ancient religious rites and even invoke the Classical gods themselves. Not everyone involved has faith in the validity – or even the sanity – of this mission, and the trip eventually involves dangerous practical jokes, seduction, murder and chicanery. Mysterious events keep happening such as the appearance of an extra statue at an ancient site or the apparent transformation of snakes devoted to Aesculapius into English garden adders. In the unravelling, we discover that the tricks were actually engineered by the Classicist himself in an attempt to persuade the others of the truth of his brand of religious archaism. However, one potentially uncanny apparition remains unexplained. Sir Rudri himself did not witness it, but one mysterious figure seen by other members of the party is not accounted for, leaving the possibility open that something magical and pagan did take place on the expedition. During these escapades in Greece, the novel sets up insistent parallels between the setting and England, and between the British characters and the figures of Classical myth and literature. At dawn, Mrs Bradley realizes she has been thinking of the land around them as if it were England: 'The great walls had been companionable; the cow a pantomime animal; the little adventure of Dick's tumbling into the pit an incident far removed from the terrors which

---

[122] Jane Garrity, *Step-Daughters of England* (Manchester: Manchester University Press, 2003), cited in Gibson, *Rediscovering Renaissance Witchcraft*, p. 51.

lived in the plays of Aeschylus.' However, 'at dawn, and, even more, she knew, beneath the hot noonday sun, Mycenae came into her own. Her tragedy and her greatness loomed like battle on the landscape'.[123] A similar surprise happens, though with the threat in the other direction, when the (apparently) harmless Greek snakes procured for the rituals are swapped for English adders. Britain glimmers through the reality of Greece in moments of transformation and shadow and British characters slip into Classical roles. The murderer turns out to be a young Englishwoman who killed a man who had been harassing her and to whom her father intended to marry her as a way to solve his professional problems. The fact that she used a bow completes the set of echoes suggested by the text: she is Artemis revenging herself on Actaeon, an Iphigenia who refuses to be sacrificed, and Mrs Bradley even sees her as Clytaemnestra.

The detective herself is likewise constructed as a figure living both in the Classical and English worlds. On encountering one of the swapped snakes, she responds by an address to the appropriate deity: '"Hail, Aesculapius," said Mrs Bradley politely, thinking it best to be on the safe side in placating the deity which, so far as she knew, still ruled in the stony valley.'[124] She then traps it gently in a suitcase and lies down to rest with her head on it. Her ease and familiarity with the deity and his symbol calls attention to her profession: that of psychoanalyst. She is a modern form of the priest healers of the Classical world undertaking a contemporary form of dream divination by applying Freudian theory. Her inhabiting of this persona for therapeutic purposes comes to a crescendo when Rudri appears to become obsessed with the idea of child sacrifice, and she worries for the safety of the boys in the party. She begins by distracting with him technicalities: '"Billets of wood," said Mrs Bradley clearly, in a practical, pleasant voice. "You've forgotten the olive wood, child."'[125] She then becomes more forceful, taking on more of the language of the Classical world, demanding 'where . . . are your billets of wood for the altar, your wine, and your five-pronged forks? Is this the manner in which you make sacrifice to the Far-Darter Apollo, you wretched, ignorant man?'[126] Finally she takes on the persona of a priestess to avert his violent obsession and she apparently employs another psychoanalytical technique by mildly hypnotizing him:

> In the sunset light of the wild glen of the Atrides she stood before him like some ancient prophetess and waved her skinny arms and menaced him with her hideous, leering lips. Her black eyes, reddened, it seemed, by the last rays of the sun, the declining Apollo, held his, and he felt he could not take his gaze from hers.[127]

---

[123] Mitchell, *Come Away*, p. 15. [124] Mitchell, *Come Away*, p. 120.

[125] Mitchell, *Come Away*, p. 142. [126] Mitchell, *Come Away*, p. 142.

[127] Mitchell, *Come Away*, p. 143.

Thus both the (sympathetic) murderer and the detective are readable through the lens of the rational detective story and through the supernatural or mythical roles of Classical myth and literature. Indeed, in this novel, Mrs Bradley's role as psychiatrist and detective seems to require that she shift between the two worlds fluently as and when it becomes necessary. *Come Away, Death* establishes the double vision characteristic of the witchy detective novel, but it does so with two variations: the foreign setting and the insistently Classical supernatural elements. In Mitchell's later developments in this mode, the former would alter as her characters found England just as enchanted as Greece, but the emphasis on the Classical world would not.

The Worsted Viper (1943) takes the Norfolk Broads as its uncanny landscape whilst developing further two images which emerged in *Come Away, Death*: Mrs Bradley as equivocal pagan priestess, and a young woman as Classical avenger. The story begins with threats made against Mrs Bradley by a group apparently involved in black magic. She is then called away to the Broads by a group of three young women (whom she previously met as study mates at the college in *Laurels Are Poison*) who have embarked on a boating holiday and found a dead body. Further murders ensue and Mrs Bradley reveals a group of practitioners of the Black Mass, one of whom has been murdering the prostitutes they hire as acolytes in their rites. This group represents the negative possibilities of the pagan and witch practices in midcentury as Sir Rudri did in *Come Away, Death*. It is never entirely clear whether the leaders of the group have a genuine belief in their form of Satanism, whether it is simply a cover for the exploitation of the vulnerable and the credulous, or whether it began as one and became the other.

Late in the novel, Mrs Bradley and her companions infiltrate one of the group's rituals (though not, the novel is careful to stress, a full Black Mass). The lengthy account includes this relatively sinister passage:

> The knife she placed on the recumbent figure of the girl upon the table, and then retired again. The white cock fluttered and squawked, as though some instinct warned it of its approaching demise. Some of the spectators shivered, but with a kind of unhealthy, erotic excitement, it seemed to Mrs Bradley; certainly not from fear.[128]

However, the ritual is also described as having 'nothing obscene about it, and nothing unpleasant', with the girl on the altar having 'the sculptured coldness of a sixth-century stele'.[129] As part of her infiltration, Mrs Bradley disguises

---

[128] Gladys Mitchell, *The Worsted Viper* (London: Michael Joseph, 1943, repr. London: Severn House, 1980), p. 158.

[129] Mitchell, *Worsted*, p. 159.

herself as an acolyte then chloroforms the priest at a crucial moment and replaces him in the ritual. She improvises 'her own ritual words – scraps from Orphic worship, sentences from the ancient ritual of the Phrygian mysteries, recollections of the religion . . . of the Minoan mysteries of Crete', also including literary sources such as Aristophanes and Hesiod.[130] As in *Come Away, Death*, the detective manages to enter the symbolic world of those who believe in (and even practice) dangerous rites and turn them into a harmless channel for the moment. Her performance is equivocal in that it is directed towards good but shows her mastery of the sinister side of the esoteric.

A more unequivocally positive kind of enchantment is provided in *The Worsted Viper* by three young women. The novel indulges in mingled scenes of idyll and adventure featuring them, rather reminiscent of Jerome K. Jerome's *Three Men in a Boat* and Arthur Ransome's *Swallows and Amazons*, if transposed to a more dramatic and magical key. Laura (who later in the series becomes Mrs Bradley's secretary) is a particular focus for the other women's attention, both for her adventurous nature and for her physicality:

> Alice handed it over, hypnotized, as usual, by the spectacle of Laura in action, for, whilst she spoke, Laura took off shirt, socks, slacks and jersey, and lightly but sufficiently clad in her vest and knickers, put the penknife, open, between her teeth and waded into the water at a point where the bank sloped down into oozy mud.
> 'The woman who braved all', she remarked as articulately as she could.[131]

She is later described as 'reclining on the cabin-top in a two-piece bathing suit' which is 'aesthetically passable, for she had a splendid body and a good skin', but '"apt to render the *embonpoint*", as Kitty euphemistically expressed it'.[132] The dual fascination of Laura's physical presence eventually becomes a dramatic part of the novel's climactic chase sequences. The leaders of the cult, including an unfrocked priest named Copley, have kidnapped one of the girls. Vengeance appears from the waters of the Norfolk Broads:

> But almost as soon as he had spoken, over the stern of his yacht swarmed a naked figure. It rose behind Copley and smote him on the base of the skull. He did not even cry out, but slithered in a heap to the side, over which vengeful Aphrodite, in the person of Laura Menzies, thrust him in a stevedore fashion which his temporarily inanimate body could not resist.[133]

The same waters from which Laura the vengeful Aphrodite appears are the means by which the other villain meets his death a page later. He is stranded by a lack of wind whilst trying to escape on another boat and 'was seen to stand

---

[130] Mitchell, *Worsted*, p. 162. [131] Mitchell, *Worsted*, p. 27. [132] Mitchell, *Worsted*, p. 85.
[133] Mitchell, *Worsted*, p. 190.

squarely on deck and invoke the breathless heavens with his cap', a practice identified by Mrs Bradley as 'setting his cap for a wind' and attributed by her (and a footnote from Mitchell) as done by King Erik of Sweden.[134] The elements appear to respond to this charm, as 'there sprang up an astonishing freak wind which ... bellied the sails of the yacht' before 'the powers of light were avenged on the representative of darkness' as it blows the boat into capsizing and he is drowned.[135] The world of dangerous occultism is symbolically rejected and destroyed by the natural world via the element in which the young women have been indulging their unusual form of pastoral.

The enchanted English pastoral is developed in an even more elaborate form in *Death and the Maiden* (1947). An unpleasant character called Mr Tidson claims to be looking for a water nymph along the banks of a river near an English cathedral. In fact he is using this as a pretext for his own criminal misdoings, including murder. Mrs Bradley, Laura and Alice become involved in the case. At one point, Alice believes she has seen the legendary naiad on the river. The resulting passages require extensive quotation to give a sense of the emotional texture and weight of words.

> Alice stood still.
>
> 'Good heavens! Do you see what I see?' she exclaimed. 'Do look! The water-nymph!'
>
> Mrs Bradley glanced, stared, looked at the surrounding reeds and willow trees, and then again at the water. A splendid, naked figure, firm, buxom and rosy, had just dived over a great clump of flowering rushes, and, entering the water like a spear-thrust, had left nothing but the widening ripples and the half-echo of a splash to convince the watcher that they had not been mistaken.
>
> Alice had clasped her strong and biting fingers on Mrs Bradley's wrist. She now disengaged them, and, bending low, began to stalk the water-nymph, losing sight of the river in her anxiety to remain unseen.[136]

Mrs Bradley has worked out that it is in fact Laura (now her secretary) rather than the naiad in the river and meets her at a pool further down.

> Laura squelched in soft mud up to the shallows, walked deeper, leaned confidently forwards, and gently re-entered the pool. Then she climbed to the rail of the bridge, balanced, first precariously and then with confidence there, drew breath and filled her deep lungs, flattened an already flat belly, soared like the sail of a yacht and took off with the flight of a swallow.

---

[134] Mitchell, *Worsted*, p. 191.   [135] Mitchell, *Worsted*, p. 191.
[136] Gladys Mitchell, *Death and the Maiden* (London: Michael Joseph, 1947, repr. Vintage, 2010), p. 122.

> Meanwhile the over-sensitive Alice had abandoned her writhings through mint, forget-me-not, moon-daisies, purple loosestrife and fool's parsley, and now came on to the path and up to the bridge.
>
> 'Well, I'm dashed,' she said, at the sight of the naked Laura. 'Here, Dog, wait for me!' In a wriggle, a squirm and a couple of heaving thrusts she was out of her clothes, and two seconds later she had entered the six-foot pool, an arrow of thin, pale light, like a willow wand newly-peeled or the sound of a silver trumpet.[137]

The whole novel slows down for these pages, moving into a rhapsodic rhetoric where lists of plants and details of the young women's bodies occupy swathes of text. Very little actual action takes place, but the intensity of description and the emphasis on Mrs Bradley's watching of the two of them register the scene as particularly significant in the novel's overall meanings. The scene ends with another description of the natural surroundings, which hints at the cosmological scale of the pastoral scene:

> The risen sun flung gold upon the shallows of the water, but the deep pool kept its shadow and greenish gloom. Larks ascended. The sky began to deepen and grow nearer. It was by this time intensely blue, and gave promise of the finest day of the summer. A breeze, very soon to die away and give place to intense and vital warmth, began to stir among the leaves of the willows, and the world was again composed of water, the air, and the sun, as it had been at the time of Creation.[138]

At the end of the novel, Mrs Bradley and Laura receive news that Tidson, whom they failed to bring to justice, has gone abroad with his family. The bodies of Tidson and his daughter Crete have been 'recovered from deep water at the end of the Mole at Santa Cruz'.[139] The novel comments that the bodies were 'locked in each other's arms in a grip that was not the clasp of love'.[140] There is a strong implication that Crete has taken vengeance for Tidson's crimes and sacrificed herself in the process. Crete takes the role of a naiad, but in a more threatening and implacable aspect. On hearing of the bodies being discovered, Laura's mind goes back to the river idyll in another remarkable passage of pastoral which ends the novel:

> 'Well, I'm glad it didn't happen in Winchester' and her blue-grey eyes saw in retrospect the grey Cathedral, the hills and the lovely darkening reaches of the river.
>
> The prospect widened and grew as clear as a vision. She saw willows and the tall, green reeds, the patches of weed, the clear and stony shallows, the uncertain deeps; the rough and thick-leaved water-plants by the brink, the

---

[137] Mitchell, *Maiden*, p. 123.   [138] Mitchell, *Maiden*, p. 123.   [139] Mitchell, *Maiden*, p. 264.
[140] Mitchell, *Maiden*, p. 264.

blue forget-me-not, the toffee-brown water-dropwort; and in side-stream and carried, ditch and brook no less than in the broadly-curving river, over the weir and under the little bridges, the smooth, hard rush of the water.

She saw the mallard in flight and the moorhens' nests built on flotsam; the scuttling dabchicks, the warblers swinging on the sedge; she saw the lithe stoat slinking swiftly back to his home; the swans like galleons for beauty; and, last, a solitary trout in a small deep pool, as he anchored himself against the run of the stream.[141]

These final paragraphs, both by their subject and by the shift back into the rhapsodic and pastoral rhetoric, recall the scenes in which Mrs Bradley watched Laura and Alice swimming in the river. The same air of enchantment is evoked, linking Crete and her death with the vision of the naked young women glorying in their physicality in the water. It shades and darkens that earlier scene whilst emphasizing the parallel world of naiads and water magic which can be seen alongside (or through) the events of the mundane world depicted in the narrative. Ironically, Mr Tidson used a hunt for a water nymph he did not believe in as the cover for his own criminal purposes and those crimes were revenged by a naiad he met in the water. This novel demonstrates the enchanted woman-centred pastoral Marsh developed in its most dramatic form. As I noted when discussing Marsh's novels, the reader is not obliged to indulge the idea that magical or mythical figures can be seen alongside the events in the 'real world'. Nonetheless, so much of the novel's emotional tone and rhetorical energy is bound up in these potentially supernatural elements that it makes more sense of the book to give these elements some weight. It is striking that Mitchell's most elaborate form of the enchanted world combines the supposedly 'feminine' turn of midcentury British writing with a focus on the English landscape.

After the water-nymph pastoral of *Death and the Maiden*, Mitchell wrote three books in which the English landscape was explored via earth and descent rather than via water and flowing. I will spend less time drawing out their rhetorical and narrative elements and summarize them more briefly than the novels discussed so far. They do not require such a careful tracing of their symbolic resonances, but they are still worth noticing as significant examples of both the witchy double vision and Mitchell's fascination with finding enchantment literally within the English landscape. *The Dancing Druids* (1948) begins with cross-country runners moving through a rural area, with the perspective character choosing a route across an Iron Age hill fort which also contains the remains of a Roman camp, allowing him to look down on the countryside before running down into it. As with the riverside idyll of *Death and the Maiden*, the surroundings are described in lengthy and atmospheric detail, but in this case,

---

[141] Mitchell, *Maiden*, p. 264.

the eerie and foreboding elements of the location are stressed. As the landscape is explored by the characters, the focus becomes a set of standing stones which give the book its title. The image is again expounded via a reverie attributed to Laura:

> Who knew, she wondered, what ghastly sights and sounds the stones had been witnesses of in long-past times and under the ancient sky? Why, anyway, were they called Druids, and, again, why should they dance? She saw them, enveloped, like witches, in cloaks of mist. She saw them writhe out of the ground, and, with slow contortions, shuffle towards their victims, avid for blood.[142]

A number of crucial events play out around the stones, including the burial of some body parts, the discovery of previous victims' burials and 'some crack-brained society carrying out what they imagine to have been an ancient rite'.[143] Mitchell gives them a local legend, that they 'dance' at certain times of the year, backs this up with a reference by Mrs Bradley within the text to the similar story told about the Rollright Stones, and then reemphasizes it with a footnote sourcing the Rollright story to Graham Clark's *Prehistoric England*. Though *The Dancing Druids* does not present modern pagan revivalism in a serious light, it does arrange a plot in which echoes and coincidences invest the stones with a mysterious atmosphere. The 'crack-brained society' are (though they don't know it) performing a ritual above the remains of a dismembered body, though not the rites so luridly imagined by Laura when she touches a stone and imagines that they 'were alive. They lived some strange, remote life of their own' and that they 'were kept alive by human blood ... by the innocent blood of murdered men'.[144] Similarly, the digging up of body parts is interrupted by one of the stones falling onto one of the criminals, leading a character to comment that 'They're called the Dancing Druids, and one of them *did* dance. You can't get away from that.'[145]

Merlin's Furlong (1952) revisited this cluster of interests around archaeology, ritual and what lies under the surface of the countryside. In a typically tortuous plot, a group of young men become involved with the disposal of a witchcraft doll, agree to break into a country house, break into the wrong one and discover a body. The ensuing narrative involves Mrs Bradley claiming to have had an ancestress who attended a pagan Walpurgis Night, the discovery of a stone altar in a grove of trees with a punning inscription and another society carrying out a ritual at a prehistoric site. The site is another Iron Age fort (with a Roman temple nearby), and it is Mrs Bradley who provides the reverie:

---

[142] Gladys Mitchell, *The Dancing Druids* (London: Michael Joseph, 1948), pp. 143–4.

[143] Mitchell, *Druids*, p. 143. [144] Mitchell, *Druids*, p. 144. [145] Mitchell, *Druids*, p. 239.

[E]ven in broad daylight, the place had a morbid fascination. As they pene-
trated deeper among the prehistoric Iron Age defenses, although the sun
shone brilliantly on all the surrounding country, not a single ray appeared to
illumine the vast, incredible walls and the deep, steep, stone-lined ditches . . .
Patiently she sat and brooded upon old, unhappy, far-off things and battles
long ago.[146]

This novel is more explicit about the presence – and danger – of diabolism and
ritual magic. The victim was murdered whilst part of an unsavoury magical
group run by a manipulative university don. There is another ritual performed
by folklore enthusiasts over a prehistoric site where a victim has been buried,
though with an additional twist in this case. The ritual is organized (via
blackmail) by one of the dead man's friends, so the group are unknowingly
performing a funerary or memorial rite.

The third book in this clutch is *A Hearse on May Day* (1972). A young
woman's car breaks down in a rural village and she has to stay the night. Despite
repeated warnings that female outsiders should not walk abroad on Mayerin'
Eve, she explores the village and finds a number of remarkable activities going
on. In a room in the inn, a group of people dressed as signs of the Zodiac are
holding a meeting of some ritual description. She also ventures into the cellars
of the inn, which connect with the disused church next door, and finds that there
is a custom of taking bones from there to bury in the Iron Age hill fort above the
village. A form of pagan festival is taking place on the hill and during the
evening, she meets a man disguised for the festival who performs a love charm.
These events are unwound into a familiar combination of atmosphere, authenticity and camouflage. The ritual group are not a survival from pagan times, but
a society founded by a previous squire of the village. The moving of bones from
the church to the hill may have originated in medieval times but has become
increasingly sinister in recent years. The love charm may or may not work, but
the heroine ends up breaking off her engagement and becoming romantically
attached to the man who performed it. Once again the novel displays a 'descent'
of various kinds into the rural landscape and the history it represents. In that
landscape, the characters and reader meet not only the traces of the past, but
those who have also attempted to revive it, for better or worse reasons.

After this sequence of novels (interspersed in Mitchell's other works) which
explore the possibilities of enchantment and double vision comes a novel which
seems to deliberately deny that vision. In *Nest of Vipers* (1979), the combination
of magic and lesbian attraction recurs, in a bleaker tone than *Death and the
Maiden* and *The Worsted Viper*. The 'vipers' of this title are a group of people

---

[146] Gladys Mitchell, *Merlin's Furlong* (London: Michael Joseph, 1953, repr. Lyons, CO: Rue
Morgue Press, 2010), p. 114.

who live in a converted mansion, a number of whom are involved in an unpleasant variety of 'black magic'. As with *Worsted Viper*, the rites involve vulnerable young women and result in murder. The novel does not contain the kind of natural vistas or reveries through which Mitchell's enchanted world tends to be mediated. As a result, the setting is thinner and the discussions of abusive magical rites are not counterbalanced by the presence – or even the implication – of a more positive magical reality. It is striking that both magic and lesbianism are more openly recognized and avowed in the quotidian world of *Nest of Vipers*, reflecting the significant social and religious changes that took place in the span of time covered by this study. Two of the characters – Billie and Elysée – are in a recognized if complex relationship, described by others as a couple, 'for their passionate friendship warrants, and, indeed, calls for, that description'.[147] The former adores the latter 'to what, for outsiders, was often an embarrassing degree, but which Elysée accepted with nonchalance and tacit approval'.[148] As this line implies, there is a strong suggestion that Elysée is less committed to the relationship. The status of their involvement is unclear, or at least ambiguous by later standards. They are accepted by others as a menage but, as a character remarks, 'There's still plenty of prejudice against emotional friendships between women.'[149] Later in the novel, Billie comments that after a certain incident, 'Ellie wouldn't allow me ever to see her in the bath any more. I accepted that ... Everybody has the option of privacy,' implying that their relationship involved a level of frustrated physical attraction only expressed under the guise of room-mate intimacy.[150] Laura, Mrs Bradley's secretary, is described as relieved not to be taking notes on a conversation with the couple, 'feeling (although she did not express the thought) ill-at-ease in the company of two women who were emotionally involved with one another'.[151] Given Laura's involvement in the rhapsodic episodes on the riverbank in *Death and the Maiden*, quoted earlier, this constitutes a serious shift in Mitchell's tone. Women's delight in each other as they plunge into the river has become narrowed into an infatuated room-mate being banned from watching her friend in the bath.

The reduction of the river to a bath has parallels in the water imagery throughout the novel. The main character met his ex-fiancée at a swimming pool where they both worked as attendants. She is called Niobe, leading to much humour on the subject of her moping demeanour recalling the tearful nymph of the same name. The victim in the murder plot was drowned in a bath full of

---

[147] Gladys Mitchell, *Nest of Vipers* (London: Michael Joseph, 1979, repr. Vintage, 2014), e-book loc. 322.
[148] Mitchell, *Nest*, loc. 332.   [149] Mitchell, *Nest*, loc. 576.   [150] Mitchell, *Nest*, loc. 2678.
[151] Mitchell, *Nest*, loc. 2652.

seawater, which she used to immerse herself in, instead of swimming in the sea nearby. The scale and enchantment of the water imagery seen in *Death and the Maiden* and *The Worsted Viper* has contracted, leaving a thinner and more mundane world. There are practitioners of magic in this novel, but they are an unwholesome cult who abuse young women and corrupt young men. There are few positive images of enchantment in the book, even when the existence of Wicca is gestured towards. There is a lengthy description of the cult's temple room, including 'cabbalistic designs' a representation of a goat's head and objects which sound like a chalice, an athame, a scourge and a stang.[152] These items could be interpreted as either Satanic or Wiccan, and Mrs Bradley remarks, 'Black rather than white magic, I fancy', thus implying the existence of good covens elsewhere.[153] She informs Laura that worship of the Great Mother was 'innocent enough in pre-Christian times' but later became corrupted.[154] When they discuss the enduring appeal of witchcraft and Laura comments, 'Of course, witchcraft is no longer against the law, as you said. I believe there are dozens of covens in England alone,' her employer replies, 'And numberless fertility rites outside them, although their practitioners nowadays seldom recognise them for what they are'.[155] Thus she diffuses modern witchcraft's claim to uniqueness amongst a whole raft of other human activities. Wicca, according to this line, is implicitly no more truly magical than attending a local dancehall or engaging in illicit passion at the golf club. The disenchantment, even disillusion, evident in *Nest of Vipers* is rendered all the more vivid by the elements it shares with the earlier, enchanted novels.

Conclusion

The novels I have selected here from Mitchell's considerable output offer the reader a set of double landscapes and double narratives in which figures of myth and magic are present at idyllic or tragic moments. The texture and tone of her novels are often richer and more insistent around these passages of potential enchantment, keeping open the Todorovian 'hesitation' which maintains the mood of the fantastic. This is familiar from the previous discussions of Christie, Allingham and Marsh, but Mitchell is notable for the emotional energy of her enchanted scenes. A reader who does not wish to indulge the possibility of magical patterns in the text is obliged to wade through a great deal of material in *Death and the Maiden* and *The Worsted Viper* which must seem extraneous or overcooked. Reading these narratives within an enchanted mode makes more coherent aesthetic sense of the books by accounting for the lengthy rhapsodies,

---

[152] Mitchell, *Nest*, loc. 2235.   [153] Mitchell, *Nest*, loc. 2244.   [154] Mitchell, *Nest*, loc. 1894.
[155] Mitchell, *Nest*, loc. 2290, 2291.

but it also makes better emotional sense of them. Such a reading explains the emotional energy which suffuses these scenes, which would otherwise seem excessive or unbalanced. However, as with the other novels explored in this Element, the supernatural lens is never insisted upon. When magic or paganism is codified into cultic activity, it becomes potentially dangerous or a tool for exploitation and one of the roles which Mrs Bradley undertakes is entering the symbolic world of ritual in order to save a victim. Her function as a detective hero is thus tied up (in these novels) with her ability to inhabit multiple versions of the world, or multiple systems of meaning, bringing the mechanisms of detective fiction into closer alignment with an enchanted view of reality.

Mitchell also differs from the other authors discussed in her intense focus (in some texts) on the relationships between women. The double vision of the witchy detective novel intersects here with Gibson's notion of bi-location. The ways in which witchy imagery can provide a parallel language to explore images of women's love and intimacy (in contemporary books such as *Lolly Willowes*) become part of the enchanted double vision of Mitchell's detective fiction. There is a distinction to be drawn between this aspect of her fiction and the heterosexual couples more common in Christie, Marsh and Allingham. In several of Mitchell's books, women's love for each other is part of the symbolism of enchantment. Their intertwining is made even more evident by the fact that both are apparently repudiated alongside each other in *Nest of Vipers*. The final element Mitchell displays in unusual intensity is her characters' move into the landscape. I have connected this with the turn to the domestic when it is found in Christie's *Murder Is Easy*, Allingham's *Cargo of Eagles* and Mitchell's *Off with His Head*, and it is even more powerfully articulated in Mitchell's narratives. Her main characters burrow, clamber, swim and dive below the surface of the landscape. The enchantment they find there parallels scenes from more explicitly fantastical contemporary novels such as the 'Piper at the Gates of Dawn' in *The Wind in the Willows* or Aslan's How in *Prince Caspian*.

Afterword

In this Element, I have examined the versions of the witchy detective novel in the work of Christie, Allingham, Marsh and Mitchell. I offer here some closing reflections in the approach I have taken and the possibilities it may open up for future research. I also look beyond the literary readings I have proposed and identify some ways in which the handling of witchcraft themes and topics in these midcentury novels parallels (and even prefigures) developments in Wicca and pagan witchcraft as a religious movement. Finally, I present a theory about why the witchy detective novel waned after the period I have been examining.

In the previous sections, I set the novels in the context of developing notions of witchcraft and paganism in the midcentury and the cultural change summed up as 'the turn to the domestic'. In the introduction, I stressed that the novels I discuss did not simply reflect a stable and coherent set of beliefs about witchcraft and paganism which were shared by the majority of the public. Instead, I argued that these books take part in the controversies over witchcraft's meanings and offer their own visions of it in dialogue with other texts. I have deliberately focussed attention on the rhetorical structures and symbolic potential of these texts since very little scholarship on midcentury witchcraft has paid this kind of detailed attention to the fictional texture of works which feature it. Marion Gibson's *Rediscovering Renaissance Witchcraft* crosses historical boundaries and reveals the cultural meanings and uses of witchcraft in fiction. Ronald Hutton's *The Triumph of the Moon* identifies the role played by novels which depict witchcraft in shaping public support or hostility. He even looks at the constellations of supernatural and pagan symbols present in the novels of writers as diverse as Kenneth Grahame, D. H. Lawrence and Charlotte Brontë. However, this Element has taken an approach which does not fall under either Gibson or Hutton's purview. It has investigated the internal workings of detective novels which depict witchcraft and identified a model of 'double vision' present in multiple authors' work. It has related this model both to the past resources of detective fiction as a genre, and to the attitudes to the world characteristic of witchcraft practitioners (as identified by Luhrmann.) In doing so, it has produced a framework for what would be called the theology of the witchy detective novel if the genre had emerged in other religious traditions. I suggest that this opens up avenues for new research and that this research has particular potential for two reasons. Firstly, much writing on witchcraft (including by practitioners) stresses the absence of formal dogma in its religious practice. Rituals and narratives are emphasized over statements of belief, and faith in deities can be metaphorical rather than literal. Therefore, an exploration of the ways witchcraft fiction operates around and about religious practices seems likely to deepen our understanding of their distinctive elements. Indeed, this exploration could usefully extend beyond witchcraft itself into the relationship between pagan fiction and modern religiosity more generally.

Secondly, the witchy detective novels I have explored had a huge reach and were not written either by pagan believers or by crusaders against witchcraft. This is not a study of reception or influence, but it is surely uncontroversial to state that the novels of Christie, Allingham, Marsh and Mitchell were collectively more widely read than the fiction of Gerald Gardner or even Dennis Wheatley. The witchy detective novel was more long-lasting than the Sunday newspapers which ran sensational stories about witches and more widely diffused than fiction which depicted witches in historical or fantastical genres. It provided the chance for readers to indulge in the potential meanings of witchcraft and even to enter the cognitive mode of some modern witches without taking an explicit position on witchcraft's reality. This points to the significance of understanding the relationship between witchcraft and fiction more generally.

Turning to parallels which have appeared in this Element, there are three intertwined themes especially visible in the novels which can be traced in the development of pagan witchcraft: a scepticism about male control within a self-declaredly feminist movement, a rethinking of the claims to unbroken historical continuity and a rethinking of the value and nature of initiation into covens. Of these, the most noticeable is the suspicion and hostility expressed across the novels towards male leaders of esoteric religious groups. The cults in Ngaio Marsh's *Spinsters in Jeopardy* and *Death in Ecstasy* are led by corrupt and exploitative men, as are the ritual groups in Gladys Mitchell's *The Worsted Viper* and *Nest of Vipers* and the self-consciously decadent group of dilletantes in Agatha Christie's *Murder Is Easy*. Sir Rudri in Mitchell's *Come Away, Death* is prepared to symbolically sacrifice his daughter and appears ready to literally sacrifice children at one point. This concern can be seen explicitly paralleled in some witchcraft practitioners, as a passage from Starhawk's influential *The Spiral Dance* demonstrates. Whilst discussing the influence of the 'East-West' dialogue and the rise of guru figures in Europe, she states:

> As women, however, we need to look very closely at these philosophies and ask ourselves the hard-headed critical question, 'What's in this for *me*? What does this spiritual system do for women?' Of course, the gurus, teachers, and ascended masters will tell us that, even by asking such a question, we are

merely continuing in our enslavement to the Lords of Mind; that it is simply
another dodge of the ego as it resists dissolution into the All.[156]

Less explicitly, many disagreements within the first generation of public
witchcraft practitioners focussed on the way Gardner's statements about an
unbroken tradition gave him a unique position of power in the religion.
Gardner's account of his initiation into witchcraft by Dorothy Clutterbuck
was not only a claim to be the most recent member of a small religious
movement, but also a claim to be the visible point of centuries upon centuries
of secret covens. When disagreements broke out between members of this
generation, they were often articulated in claims that one or other of those
involved was not in fact a representative of an ancient and continuous tradition, or that the material they presented was not historically authentic. For
example, Hutton relates that the catalyst for the priestess Doreen Valiente
leaving Gardner's Hertfordshire coven was his sudden production of hitherto
unmentioned traditional Laws of the Craft 'written in archaisms which seemed
to Valiente to be very clearly artificial, and she suspected them of having been
invented for the occasion' including 'clauses which limited the authority of
high priestesses and seemed to be a clear riposte to her opposition of Gardner's
policies'.[157] These controversies did not involve open disagreement about the
place of men in the movement but they do demonstrate the connection
between scepticism about powerful male figures with claims to unique knowledge and the effect of the model of an unbroken chain of covens. That
unbroken chain depended upon two principles: a continuous line of initiation
and the literal existence of the witch cult throughout history. Both came to be
questioned or relativized by later witchcraft writers. Starhawk, for example,
states that '[s]ome covens follow practices that have been handed down in an
unbroken line since before the Burning Times' whilst '[o]thers derive their
rituals from leaders of modern revivals of the Craft' including Gardner and
Alex Sanders.[158] Her commentary on the text in the late 1990s stresses that her
work is 'mythic history' and 'not a Ph.D. thesis', softening the claim that there
has been a continuous tradition with an objective content.[159] The commentary
is even less concerned with the lines of initiation, stating that initiation can
'become a badge, a mark of status', and that solitary witches are now 'the
norm'.[160] Vivianne Crowley's *Wicca: The Old Religion in the New Age* (1989)
and Doreen Valiente's *Witchcraft for Tomorrow* (1978) both insist on the

---

[156] Starhawk, *The Spiral Dance: A Rebirth of the Ancient Religion of the Great Goddess*
(New York: HarperCollins, 1979, repr. annotated ed., 1999), p. 222.
[157] Hutton, *Triumph*, p. 249.   [158] Starhawk, *Dance*, p. 35.   [159] Starhawk, *Dance*, p. 265.
[160] Starhawk, *Dance*, pp. 276, 265.

validity of Gardner's initiation and the continuity – if not the identity – of tradition, but seem to be moving in a relativizing direction. Rae Beth's *Hedge Witch* (1990) is predicated on it being possible to practice witchcraft alone and without initiation and she refers to the old religion as 'now new, reborn', and having 'evolved', but as still part of ongoing paganism across the centuries.[161]

I have made this brief excursion into later witchcraft writings because these crucial issues are also worked through in some of the witchy detective novels. The works I have been discussing take a variety of attitudes to this question of the authenticity and continuity of witchcraft traditions. *The Pale Horse* seems to unequivocally condemn the idea as a form of ignorance and superstition, particularly when re-expressed in more modern-sounding scientific terms. *Spinsters in Jeopardy* seems to regard witchcraft and occultism as an authentic tradition, but one of human folly and risk in which new generations return to the same sources in search of knowledge and power. Gladys Mitchell's work emphasizes the scepticism about initiation because of its insistent diffusing of magic and mythic images throughout the fictional landscape. The swimmers of *Death and the Maiden* and *The Worsted Vipers* possess an enchantment which does not depend upon cultic activity or organization. Even in the disenchanted *Nest of Vipers*, Mrs Bradley states that numerous fertility rites are going on outside covens. It is in Margery Allingham's work that the fullest theory of magical revival appears. As I have argued, *Look to the Lady*, *Sweet Danger* and *Cargo of Eagles* develop a dialectical model of authenticity which can be examined even at the sentence level. They depict a magic which can arise almost spontaneously in the English countryside, not because it has been passed down from initiate to initiate, but because surrounding conditions and folk traces exist which collide with the wills and purposes of the living characters. The plot of *Look to the Lady* frustrates the desire of the US professor to discover a continuous tradition of witch ritual in the depths of rural England, instead allowing him to witness the spontaneous regeneration of witchery as the dispossessed old woman draws on remembered lore to achieve the same ends as early modern witches. The novel does not suggest that her use of the goat-creature costume was fraud, and certainly not in the same category as the pretentious arty crowd who swarm around the Gyrth chalice. The three novels present authentically enchanted scenes whose authenticity does not depend on an unbroken chain of mystery or craft being passed down the centuries. Thus these authors can be seen developing their own images and theories on questions around the meaning, identity and

---

[161] Rae Beth, *Hedge Witch: A Guide to Solitary Witchcraft* (Bury St Edmunds: St Edmundsbury Press, 1990), p. 12.

continuity of witchcraft which came to be central in the ongoing development of pagan witchcraft as a religious movement.

Despite this richness of fictional vision, the witchy detective novel dwindled after the midcentury. I have sketched in previous sections the turn towards outright disenchantment in two of the authors: Christie and Mitchell. More generally, the novels which occupy the characteristic double vision fade away. The next generation of female British detective writers do not tend to create the same fictional matrix, even when they deal with similar material. Ruth Rendell's *Babes in the Wood* (2002) may invert the plot of Buchan's *Witch Wood*, but only to produce a group of unstable and dangerous Christians worshipping in the field beyond the town. The standing stones of P. D. James' *The Private Patient* (2008) are the focus of an obsessive mind, but not one whose ideas the reader can share. The Wiccan narrator and Samhain setting of Rebecca Tope's *Death in the Cotswolds* (2006) presents witchcraft as a social phenomenon rather than a mode of enchantment. I suggest that this can be explained by the changing status of witchcraft, both socially and conceptually, in the late twentieth and early twenty-first centuries. In the era covered by this study, witchcraft's legal position moved from being a technically prohibited esoteric activity to being an officially recognized form of spirituality alongside other religions. Socially and conceptually, it also moved from a set of claims about history and science to being a generally self-contained set of religious principles and practices. As seen in this Element, modern witchcraft writers are much less likely to insist on the literal historical accuracy of the claims made by Gardner and the first generation of public witches. Neither do they tend to repeat his other claims: that witchcraft and science are coming together to produce a unified form of knowledge. Rather, witchcraft has found a place as a religion in both its internal rhetoric and legal acceptance: it no longer makes attempts to alter the publicly accepted consensus view of reality. During this process, as witchcraft has moved to an epistemologically stable category as a minority religion in a pluralist society, the impetus for the witchy detective novel has disappeared. The double vision of an enchanted world where witches may or may not exist is less compelling in a world where they definitely do exist and have international conferences. In this situation, Todorov's model of the fantastic reasserts itself: any unexplained witchery in a detective novel is likely to be swiftly resolved into either an illusion or a fantasy. This theory would explain the appearance and dispersal of this mode within detective fiction but also focus attention on the genre's dynamic engagement with the continuing debates about the nature and meaning of witchcraft. By the end of the era I have explored, the long hesitation of the fantastic, which lasted several decades, had closed.

Bibliography

Allingham, Margery. *Cargo of Eagles* (London: Chatto and Windus, 1968, repr. undated), e-book.

Look to the Lady (London: Jarrolds, 1931, repr. Penguin, 1950).

Sweet Danger (London: Heinemann, 1933, repr. Penguin, 1950).

Ascari, Maurizio. *A Counter-history of Crime Fiction: Supernatural, Gothic, Sensational* (Basingstoke: Palgrave Macmillan, 2007).

Briggs, Robin. *Witches and Neighbours: The Social and Cultural Context of European Witchcraft* (Malden, MA: 2002, 2nd ed.).

Christie, Agatha. *Death Comes As the End* (London: Collins, 1944, repr. HarperCollins, 2017), e-book.

Miss Marple: The Complete Short Stories, (London: Harper Collins, 1997).

Murder Is Easy (London: Collins, 1938, repr. HarperCollins, 2017), e-book.

The Pale Horse (London: Collins, 1961, repr. HarperCollins, 2010), e-book.

Cook, Michael. *Detective Fiction and the Ghost Story: The Haunted Text* (Basingstoke: Palgrave Macmillan, 2014).

Frazer, J. G. *The Golden Bough: A Study in Magic and Religion* (London: Macmillan, 1922 abridgement, repr. 1932).

Gardner, Gerald. *Witchcraft Today* (London: Rider, 1954).

Garrity, Jane. *Step-Daughters of England* (Manchester: Manchester University Press, 2003).

Gibson, Marion. *Rediscovering Renaissance Witchcraft: Witches in Early Modernity and Modernity* (Abingdon: Routledge, 2018).

Guglielmi, Waltraud. 'Agatha Christie and Her Use of Ancient Egyptian Sources', in Charlotte Trumpler, ed. *Agatha Christie and Archaeology* (London: British Museum Press, 2001), pp.351–89.

Hutton, Ronald. *The Triumph of the Moon: A History of Modern Pagan Witchcraft* (Oxford: Oxford University Press, 1999, repr. 2001).

James, Phyllis Dorothy. *The Private Patient* (London: Faber and Faber, 2008).

Light, Alison. *Forever England: Femininity, Literature and Conservatism between the Wars* (London: Routledge, 1991).

Luhrmann, Tanya. *Persuasions of the Witch's Craft: Ritual Magic and Witchcraft in Present-Day England* (Oxford: Blackwell, 1989).

Magliocco, Sabine. 'New Age and Neopagan Magic', in David J. Collins, SJ, ed. *The Cambridge History of Magic and Witchcraft in the West* (Cambridge: Cambridge University Press, 2015), pp. 635–63.

Mann, Jessica. *Deadlier Than the Male: An Investigation into Feminine Crime Writing* (London: David and Charles, 1981).

Marsh, Ngaio. *Dead Water* (London: William Collins, 1964, repr. Fontana, 1983).

Death in Ecstasy (London: Geoffrey Bles, 1936, repr. HarperCollins, 2009).

Off with His Head (London: William Collins, 1957, repr. HarperCollins, 2009), e-book.

Spinsters in Jeopardy (London: William Collins, 1954, repr. Fontana 1986).

When in Rome (London: William Collins, 1970, repr. Fontana, 1971).

Mitchell, Gladys. *Come Away, Death* (London: Michael Joseph, 1937, repr. Penguin, 1954).

The Dancing Druids (London: Michael Joseph, 1948).

Death and the Maiden (London: Michael Joseph, 1947, repr. Vintage, 2010).

Merlin's Furlong (London: Michael Joseph, 1953, repr. Lyons, CO: Rue Morgue Press, 2010).

Nest of Vipers (London: Michael Joseph, 1979, repr. Vintage, 2014), e-book.

The Worsted Viper (London: Michael Joseph, 1943, repr. London: Severn House, 1980).

Ptah-hotep. *The Instruction of Ptah-hotep and the Instruction of Ke'gemni*, tr. Battiscombe Gunn (London: John Murray, 1906).

Purkiss, Diane. *The Witch in History: Early Modern and Twentieth-Century Representations* (London: Routledge, 1996).

Rendell, Ruth. *Babes in the Wood* (London: Hutchinson, 2002).

Rowland, Susan. *From Agatha Christie to Ruth Rendell* (Basingstoke: Palgrave, 2001).

Starhawk. *The Spiral Dance: A Rebirth of the Ancient Religion of the Great Goddess* (New York: HarperCollins, 1979, repr. annotated ed., 1999).

Todorov, Tzvetan. *The Fantastic: A Structural Approach to a Literary Genre*, tr. Richard Howard (Ithaca, NY: Cornell University Press, 1973, repr. 1975).

The Typology of Detective Fiction (1966), repr. in Chris Geer, ed. *Crime and Media: A Reader* (London: Taylor & Francis, 2009).

Tope, Rebecca. *Death in the Cotswolds* (London: Allison and Busby, 2006).

Magic

Marion Gibson

University of Exeter

Marion Gibson is Professor of Renaissance and Magical Literatures and Director of the Flexible Combined Honours Programme at the University of Exeter. Her publications include *Possession, Puritanism and Print: Darrell, Harsnett, Shakespeare and the Elizabethan Exorcism Controversy* (2006), *Witchcraft Myths in American Culture* (2007), *Imagining the Pagan Past: Gods and Goddesses in Literature and History since the Dark Ages* (2013), *The Arden Shakespeare Dictionary of Shakespeare's Demonology* (with Jo Esra, 2014), *Rediscovering Renaissance Witchcraft* (2017) and *Witchcraft: The Basics* (2018). Her new book, *The Witches of St Osyth: Persecution, Murder and Betrayal in Elizabethan England*, will be published by Cambridge University Press in 2022.

About the Series

Elements in Magic aims to restore the study of magic, broadly defined, to a central place within culture, one which it occupied for many centuries before being set apart by changing discourses of rationality and meaning. Understood as a continuing and potent force within global civilisation, magical thinking is imaginatively approached here as a cluster of activities, attitudes, beliefs and motivations which include topics such as alchemy, astrology, divination, exorcism, the fantastical, folklore, haunting, supernatural creatures, necromancy, ritual, spirit possession and witchcraft.

Cambridge Elements ☰

Magic

Printed in the United States
by Baker & Taylor Publisher Services